HEROES, HOPE, AND HIGH WATER
LIFE LESSONS IN TURBULENT TIMES

Heroes, Hope, and High Water: Life Lessons in Turbulent Timez is published under Aspire, a sectionalized division under
Di Angelo Publications, Inc.

Aspire is an imprint of Di Angelo Publications.
Copyright 2022.
All rights reseved.
Printed in the United States of America.

Di Angelo Publications
4265 San Felipe #1100
Houston, Texas 77027

Library of Congress
Heroes, Hope, and High Water: Life Lessons in Turbulent Times
Hardback
ISBN: 9781--942549-50-5

Words: Bill Baldwin
Cover Photo: Katya Horner
Cover Design: Savina Deianova
Interior Design: Kimberly James
Editors: Elizabeth Geeslin Zinn

Downloadable via Kindle, iBooks, Nook, and Google Play.

No part of this publication may be reproduced, distributed, or transmitted in any form or by any means without the prior written permission of the publisher, except in the case of brief quotations embodied in critical reviews and certain other noncommercial uses permitted by copyright law. For permission requests, contact info@diangelopublications.com.

For educational, business, and bulk orders, contact sales@diangelopublications.com.

1. Commencement Address
2. Memoir - Natural Disaster

HEROES, HOPE, AND HIGH WATER
LIFE LESSONS IN TURBULENT TIMES

BILL BALDWIN

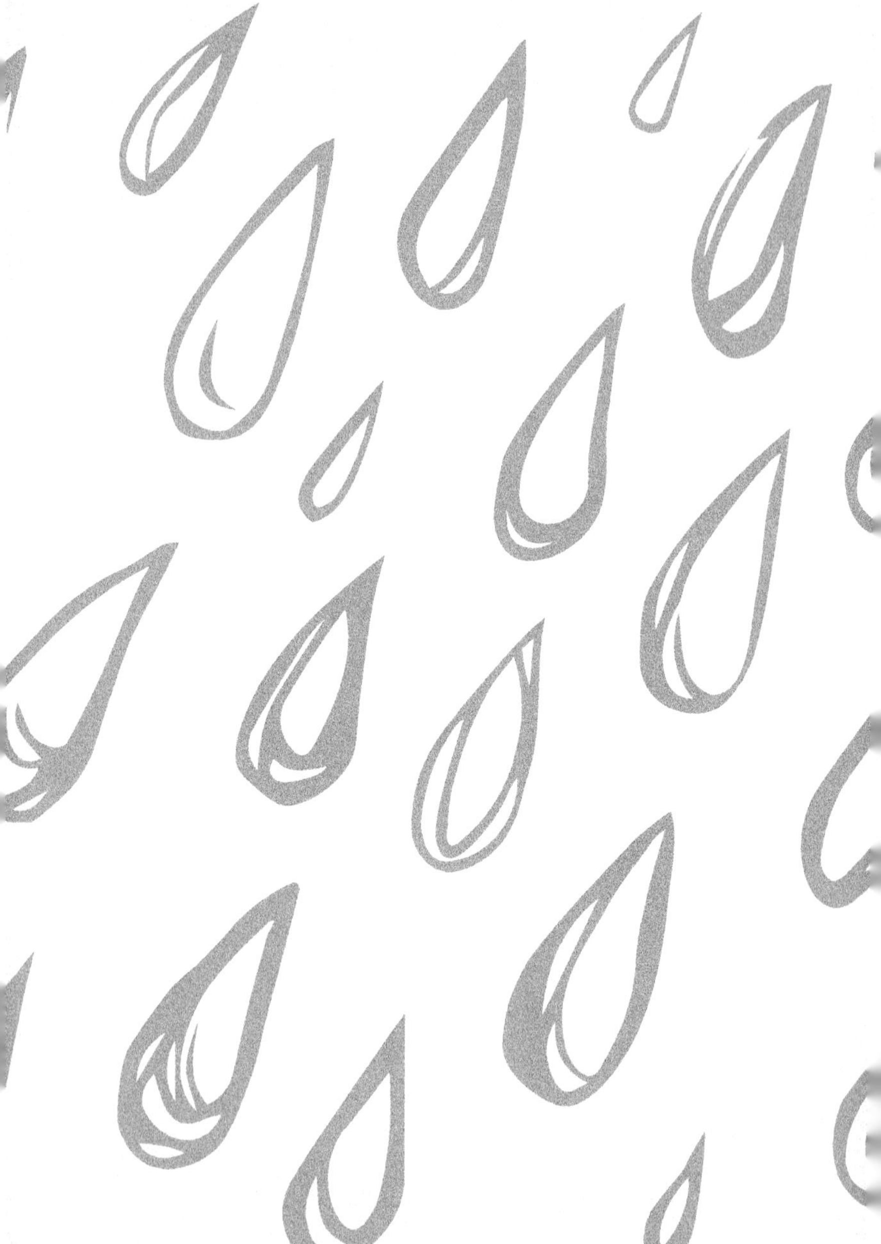

PREFACE

My partner, Fady, thinks I wrote a book about a hurricane.

I think I have written a book about what happened after a hurricane—and the goodness in mankind after an exceptional event in time.

As it has now been five years since Hurricane Harvey, it is the perfect time to reflect on those events. Since then, we have had other critical events such as the deep freeze of 2021, years of the COVID pandemic, and national elections that highlight the extreme division among people.

Seeing these events makes it easy to become discouraged and depressed.

Reflecting on the lessons mentioned in this book is now more important than ever.

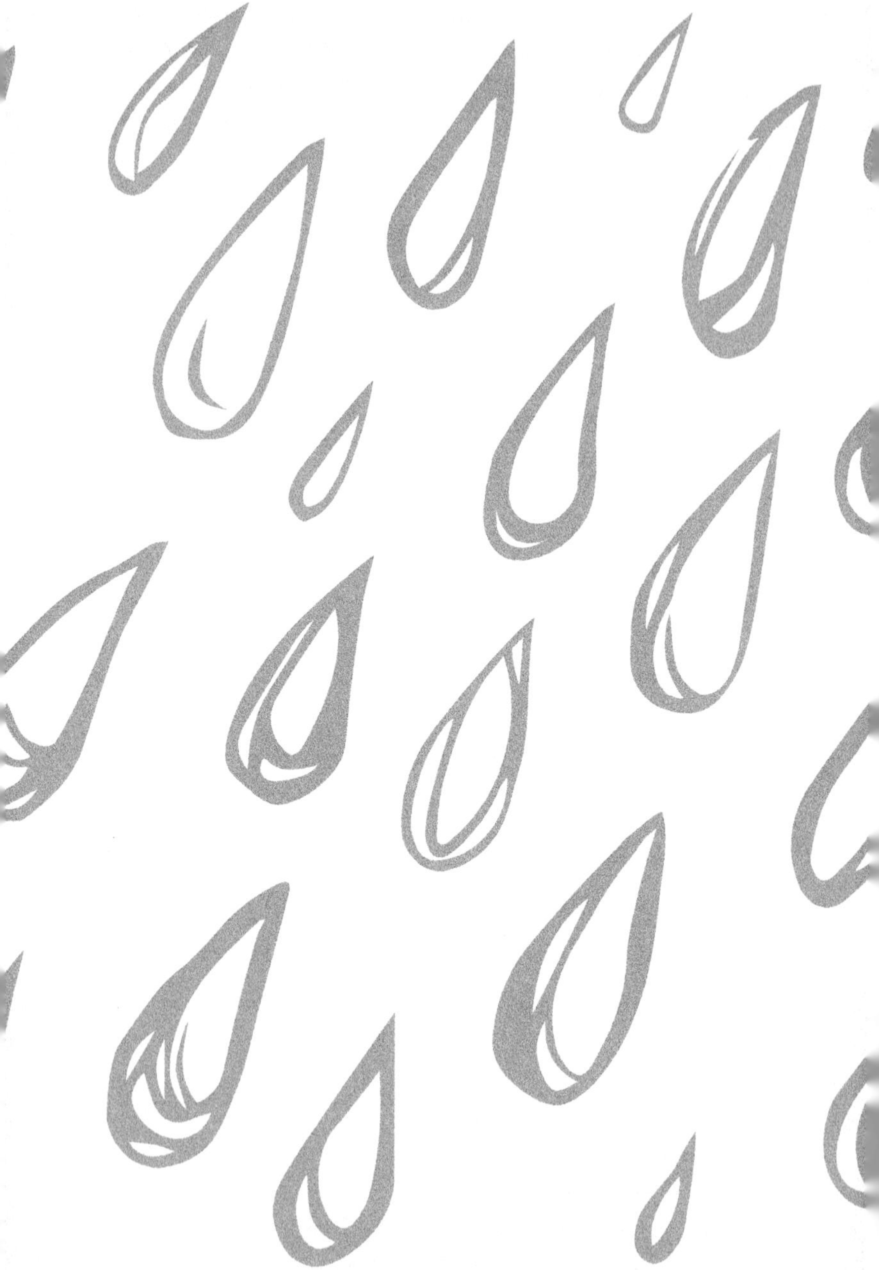

I was honored to give the commencement address at Sam Houston State University in Huntsville, Texas on August 4, 2018, the summer after the Texas Gulf Coast Region experienced Hurricane Harvey.

This book and these life lessons are the end result of that event.

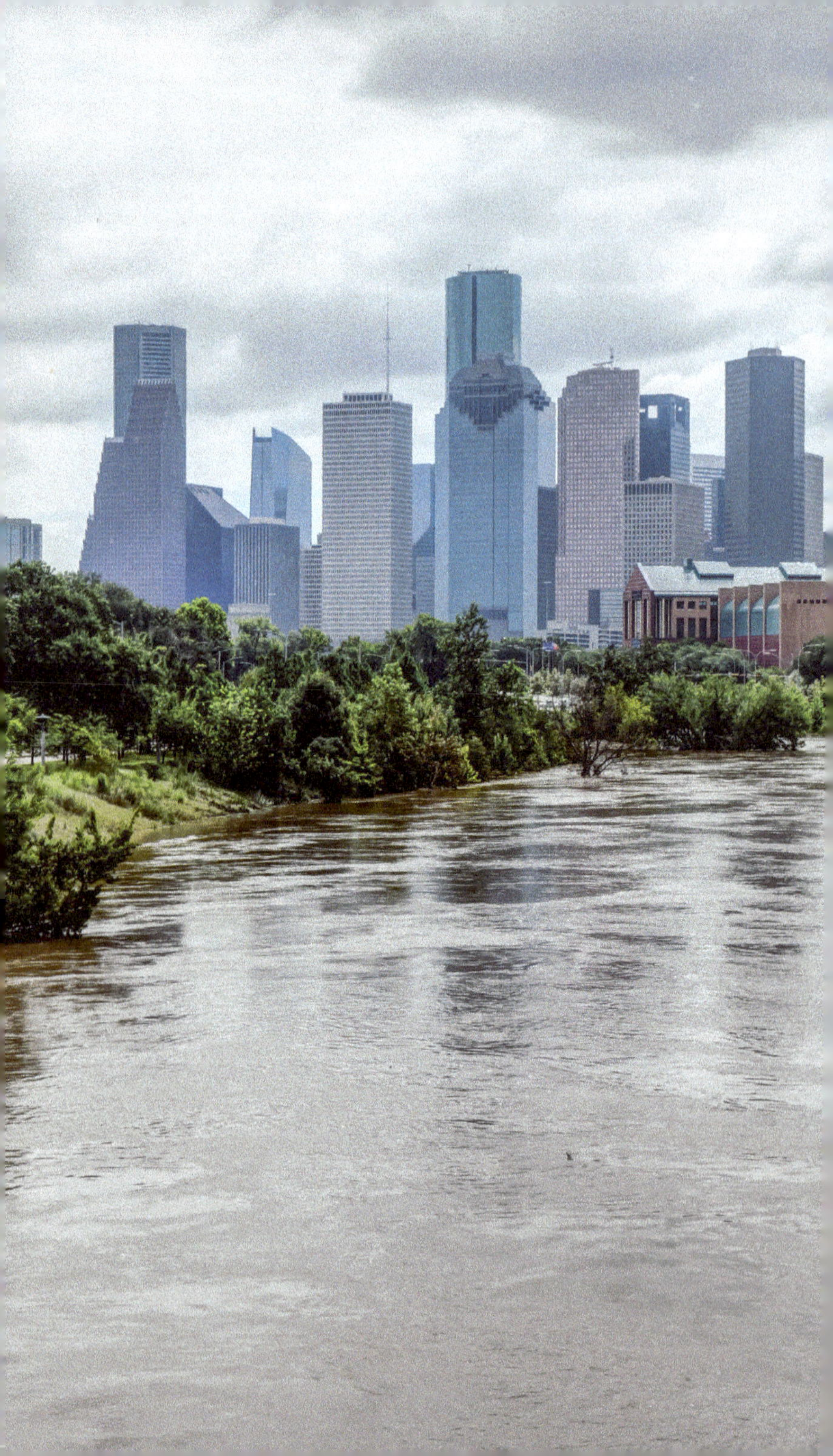

In late August of 2017, Hurricane Harvey swept across our region and disrupted the lives of *millions* of people across our state. You did not have to be flooded to have been impacted by this catastrophic event. Hundreds of thousands were flooded. Dozens died. Some were forced to evacuate their homes. Many waited for it to end—only to be flooded later by a reservoir that was designed to protect them.

I hope and pray that you were spared, but there is no doubt some of you were directly impacted or know someone who was.

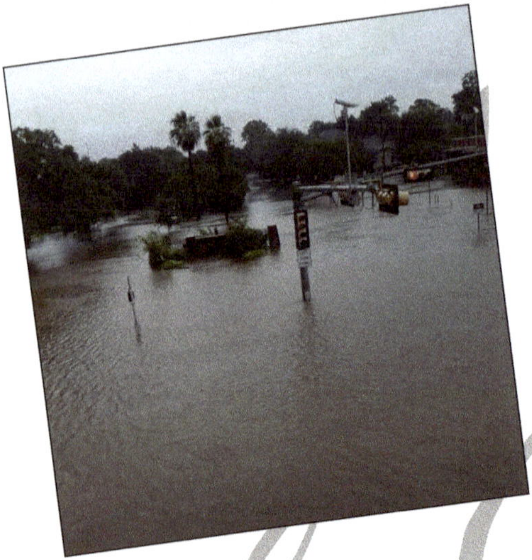

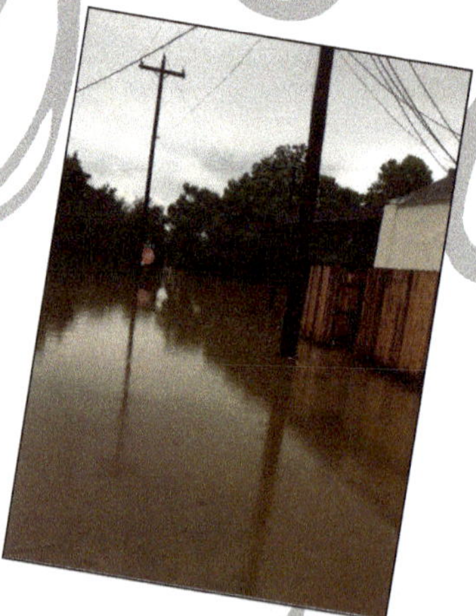

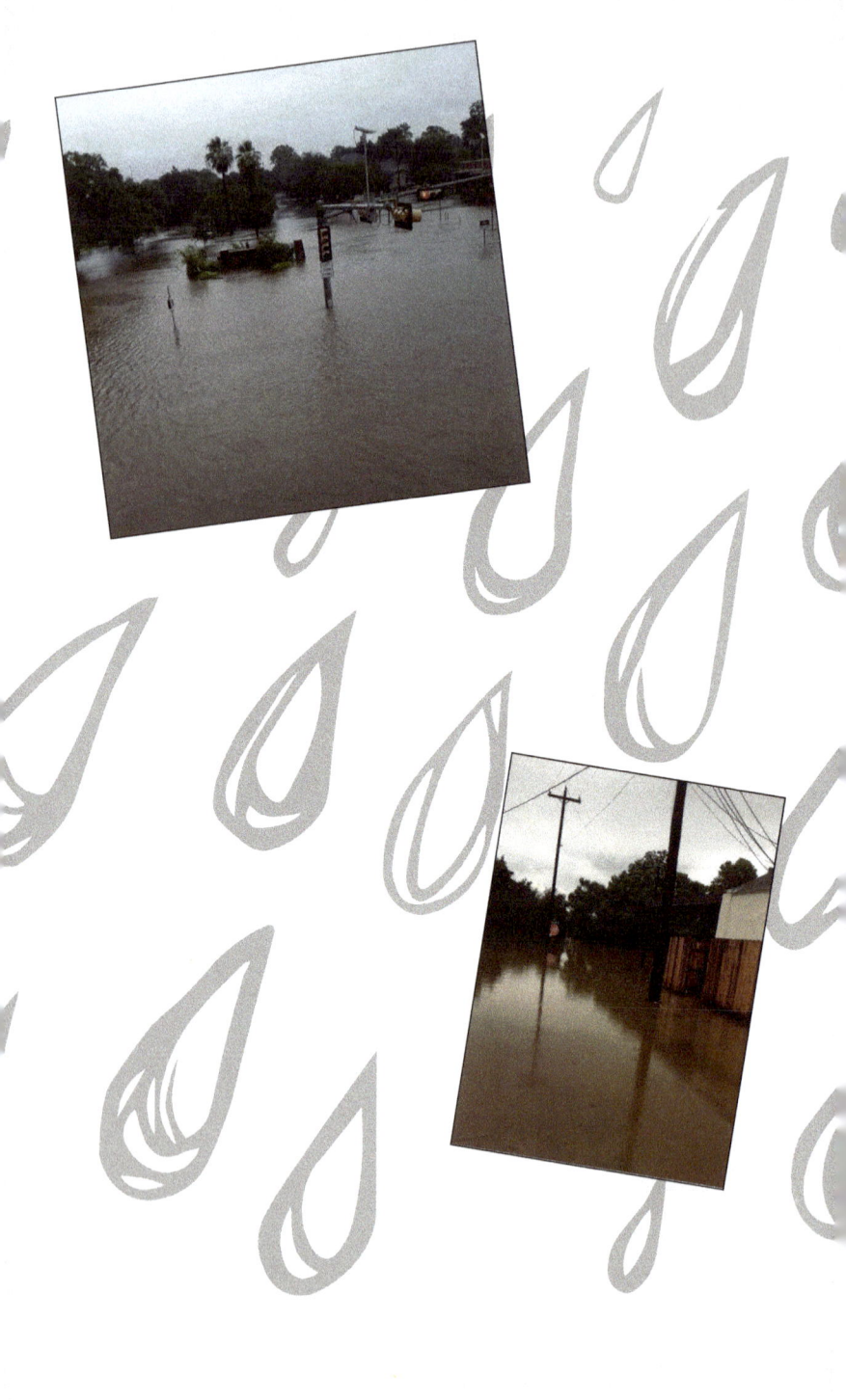

Our house had <u>no</u> flooding or damage.

My partner and I watched from the **comfort** of our home like millions of Americans did on that Saturday. We watched the devastation and destruction that crossed a vast region of our state.

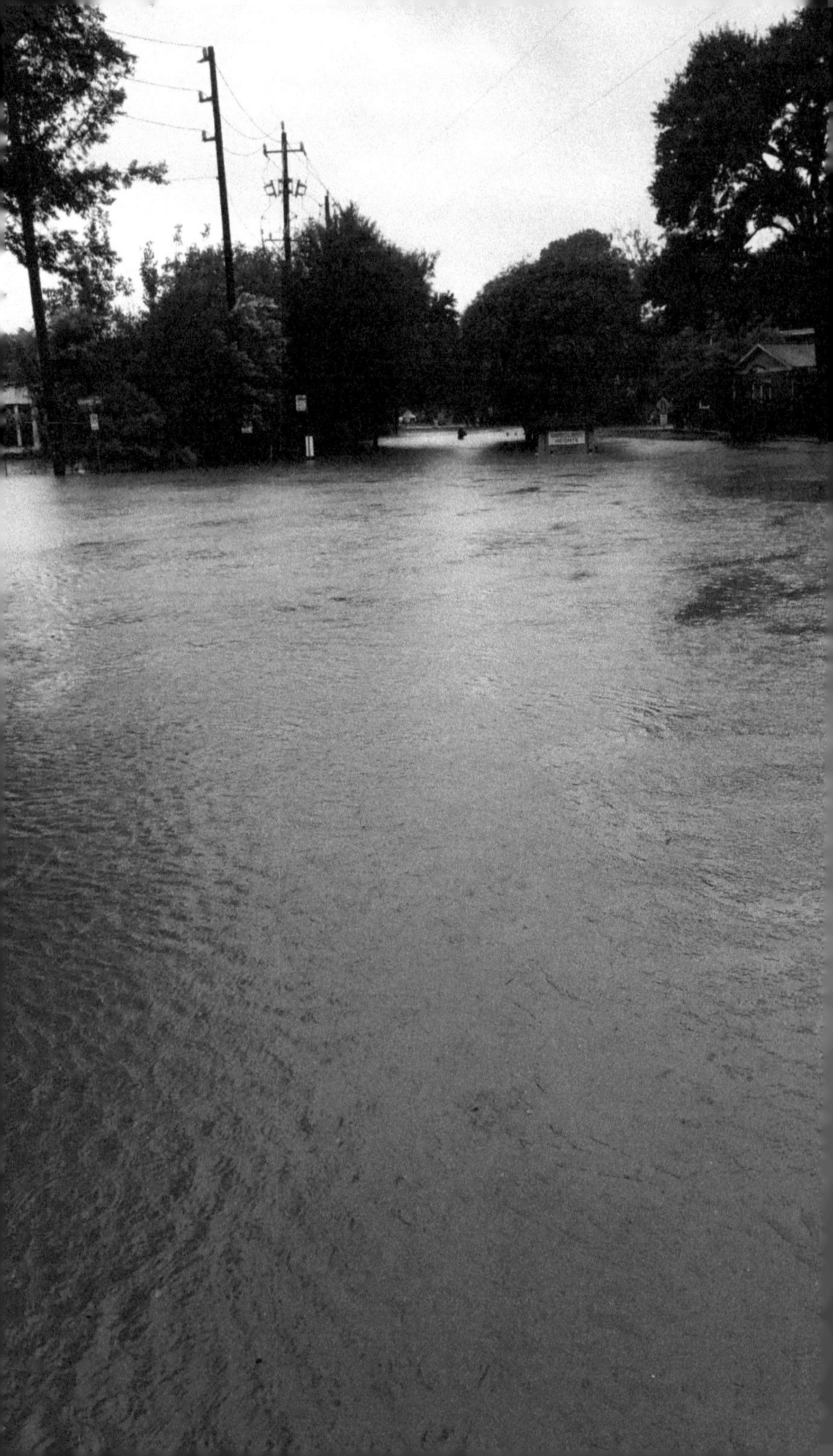

Early that next morning, after surveying our immediate neighborhood, I made a personal, yet fateful, decision to go and volunteer at the city's emergency Disaster Relief Center downtown at the George R. Brown Convention Center.

I took off on my bicycle, wading through four feet of water at one point, to get there. I could have, and most likely should have, turned around. It would have been the safe thing to do. But something deep inside me made me keep going. Something that is still hard to describe today.

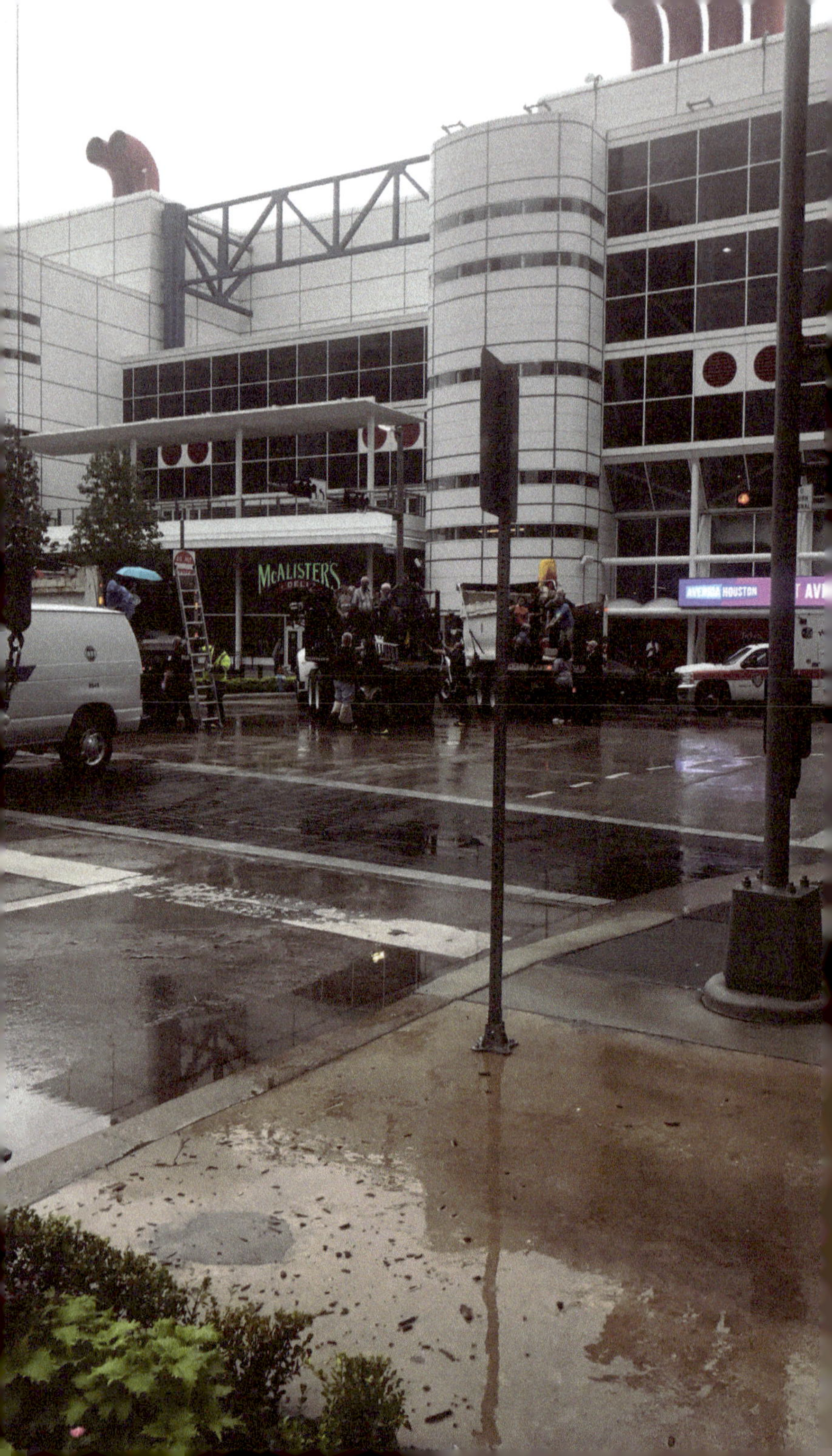
McALISTERS
DELI
HOUSTON

Upon my arrival, it was not difficult to see that the location set up to assist was still in need of assistance. By coincidence, I was put in charge of volunteer coordination that day.

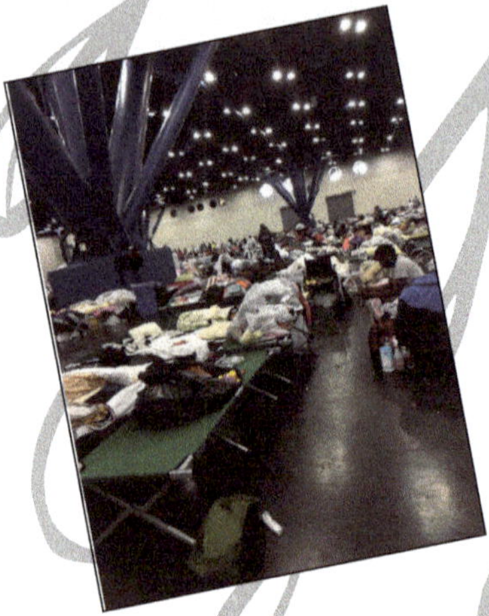

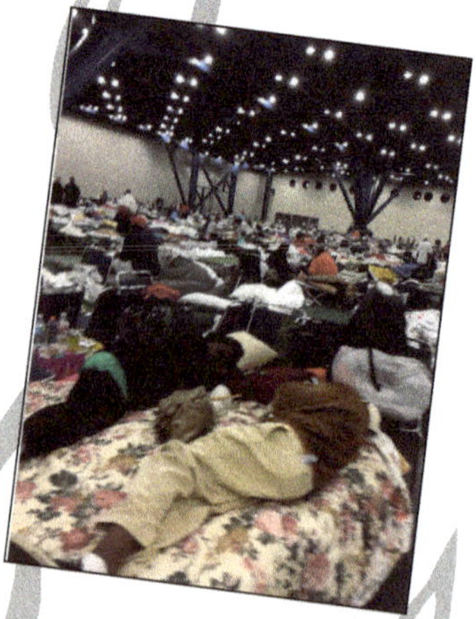

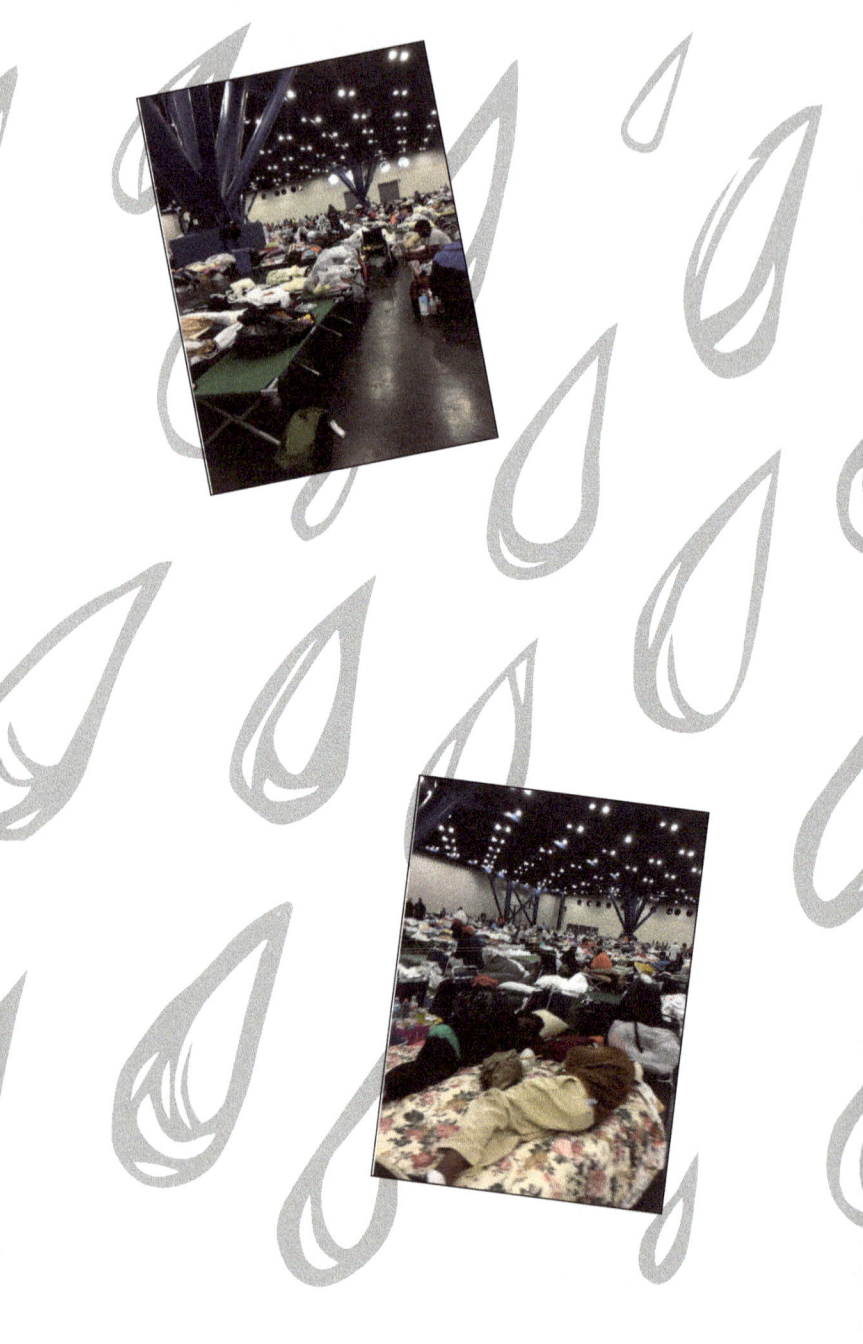

Remarkably, even before many evacuees had arrived, there were already numerous volunteers lining up to help serve.

Untrained and with little supervision, we began welcoming hundreds who were wet, cold, hungry, and disillusioned. We assembled cots. We took in families, individuals, the disabled, and even many pets. We immediately began accepting donations. There were medical needs, bathing challenges, security concerns, and mouths and souls to feed and comfort.

Over the next few days, the evacuee number rose to 15,000, and at the same time, the number of people willing to volunteer, donate, and serve continued to rise.

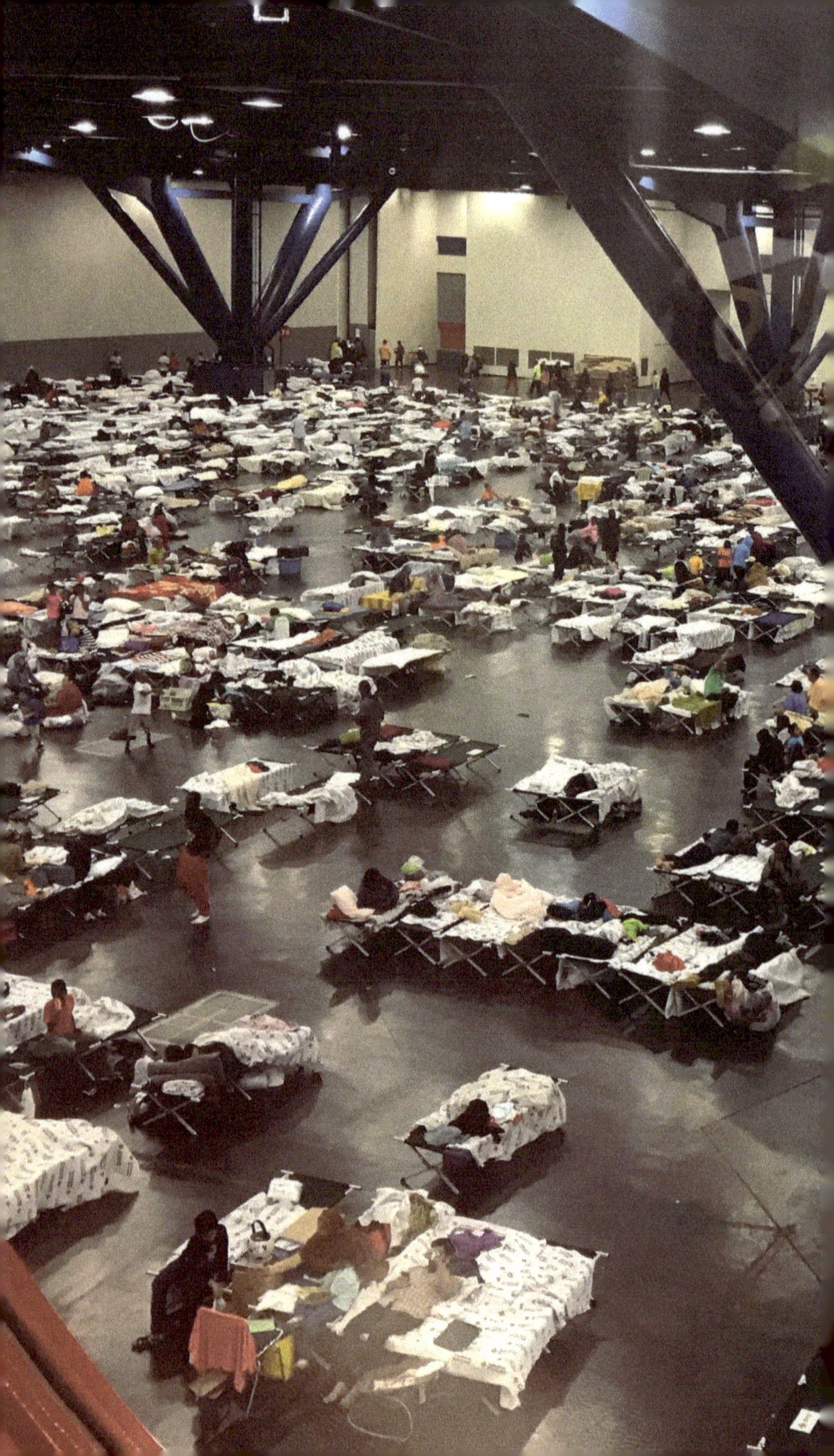

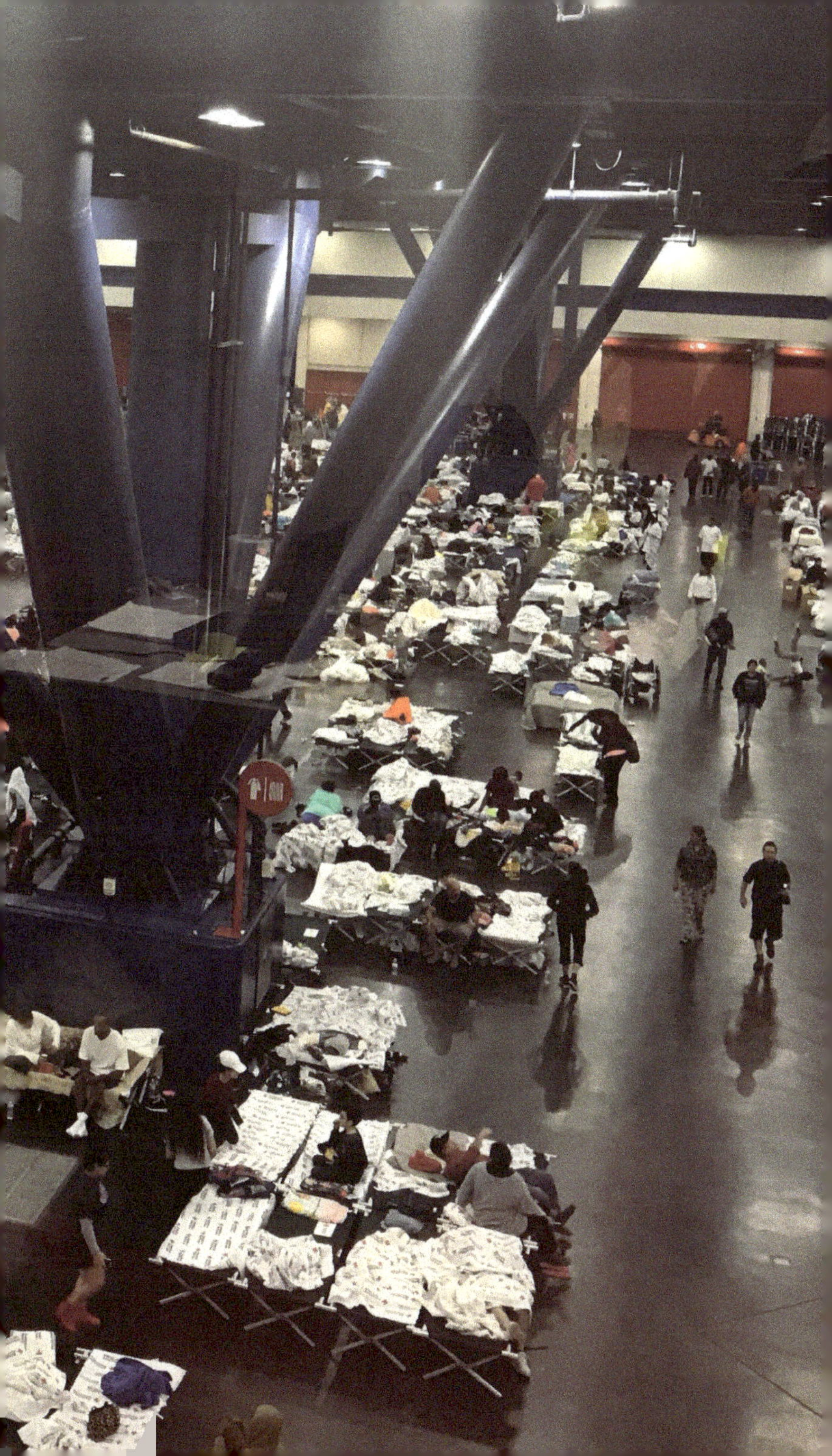

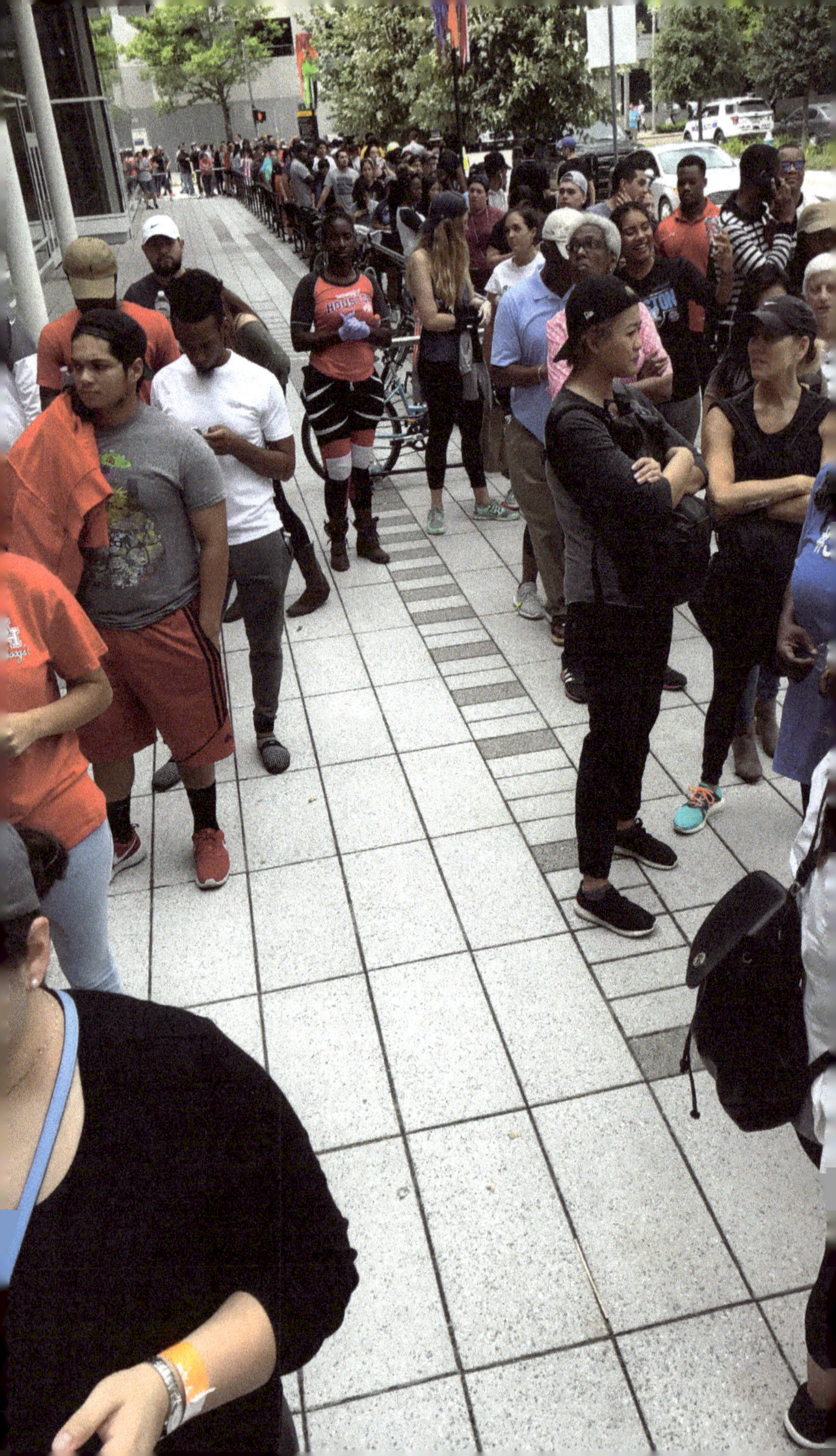

Many of those wishing
to volunteer waited
~~hours and hours~~
in line to do so, only to
be turned away as we
had more volunteers
than we could handle.

Donations became so
enormous that after
several days, there was
just no more room
for anything else, and
donations were no longer
accepted there.

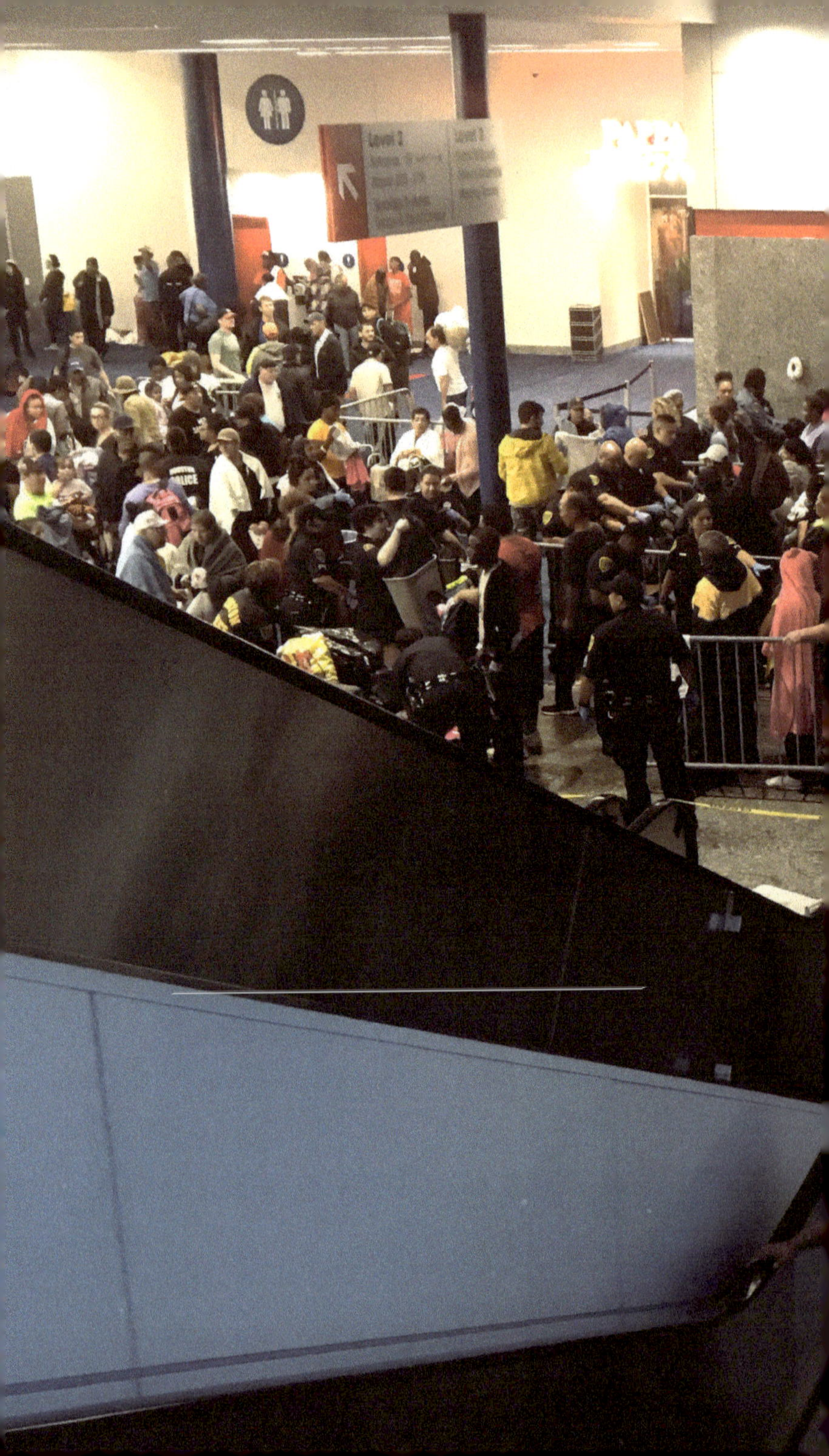

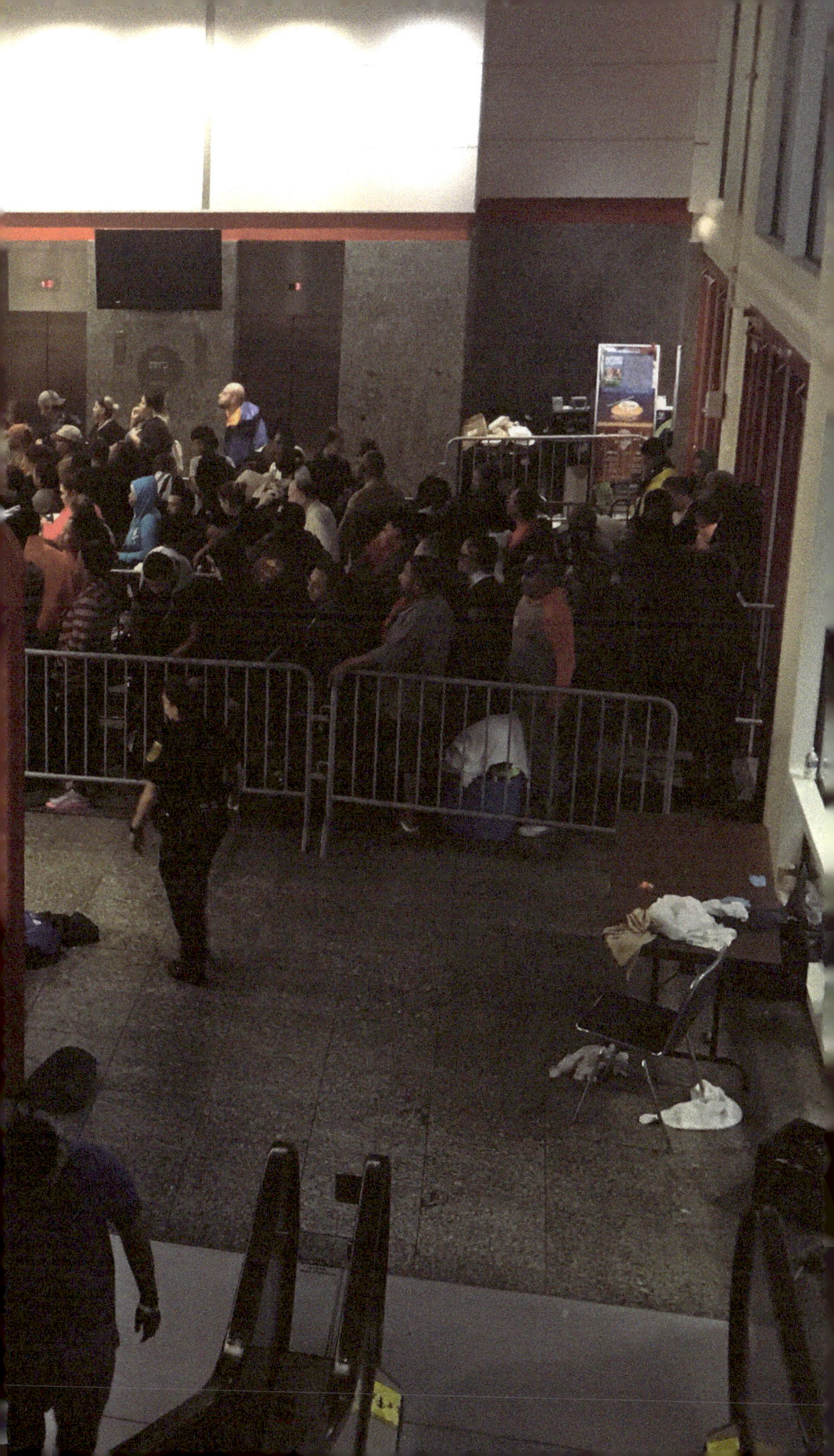

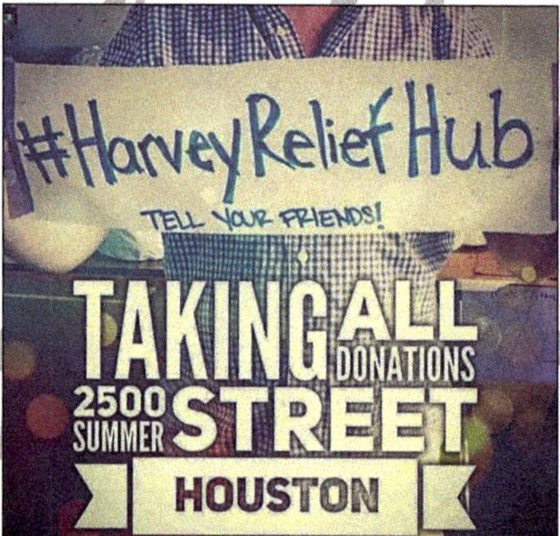
#HarveyReliefHub
TELL YOUR FRIENDS!
TAKING ALL DONATIONS
2500 SUMMER STREET
HOUSTON

Seeing the outpouring of resources available to the 15,000 people in the city and county shelters led me to question my need to be there, and I began to think about a way to serve the tens of thousands of our neighbors who were *not* in shelters.

So, after five days, I decided, along with friends I had only met there that week, to reach out with my partner and start the Harvey Relief Hub.

We would help pair together those wanting to serve, those wanting to donate, and those wanting to help in other ways, with those in need of help, supplies, and information.

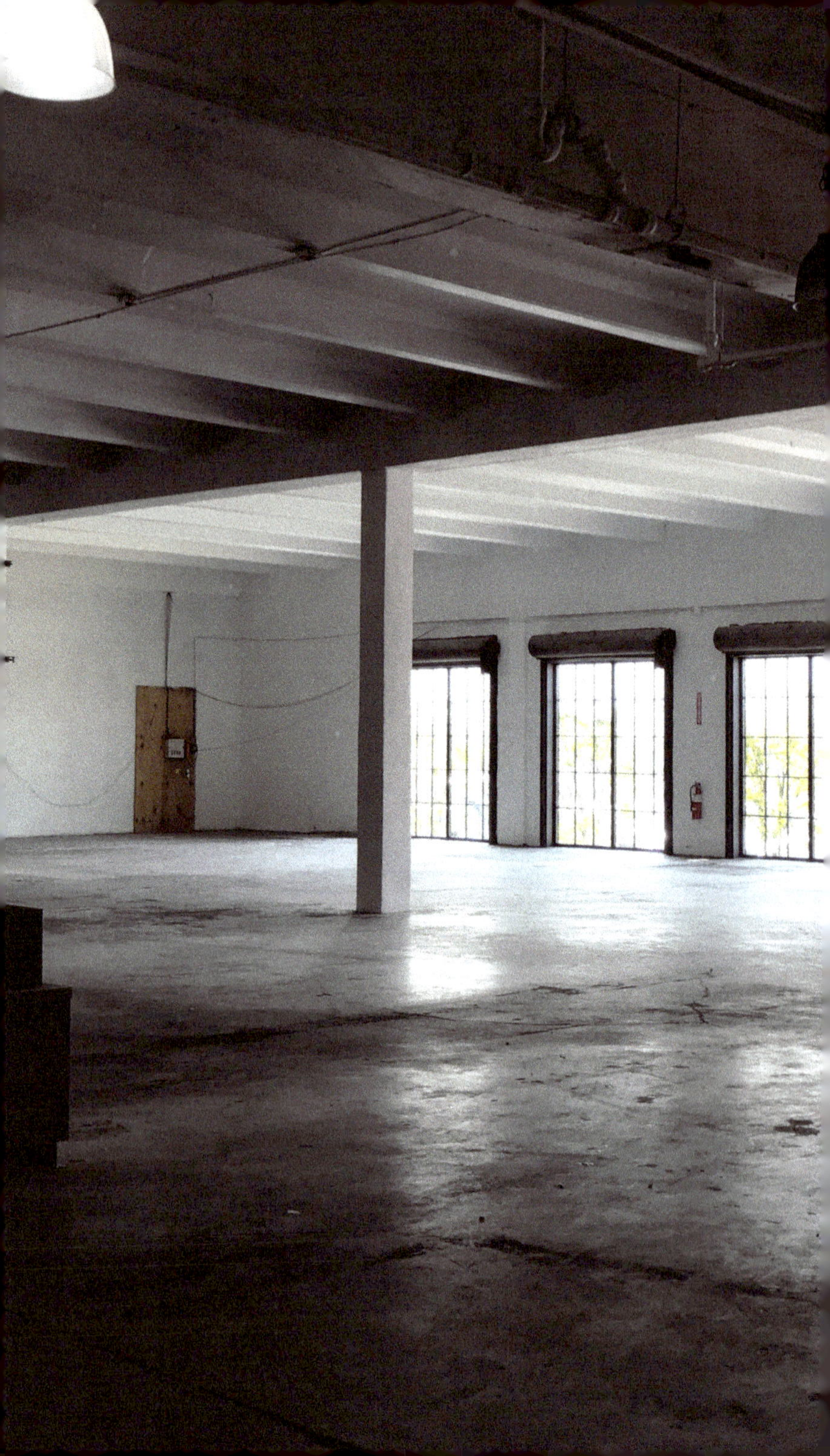

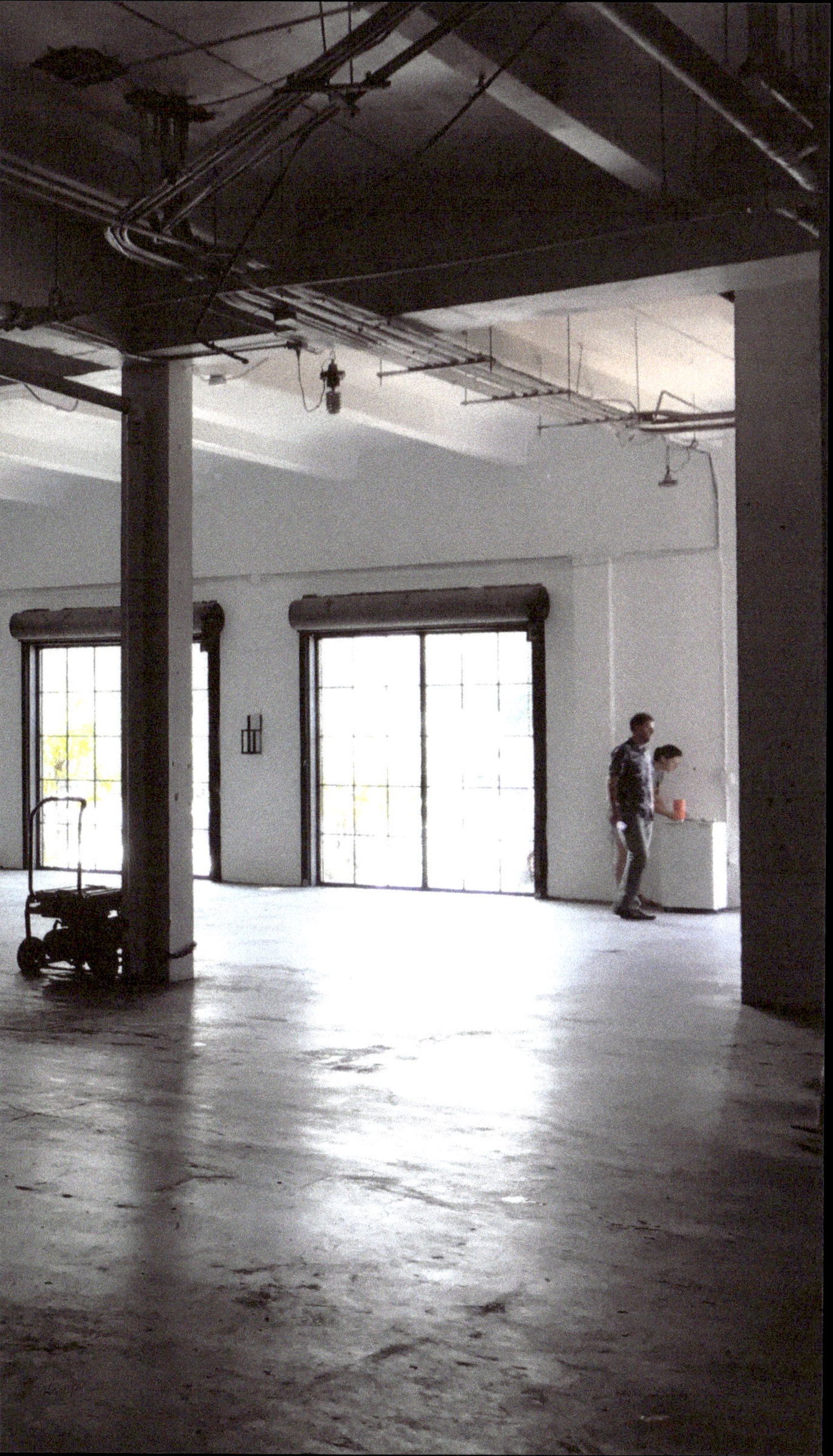

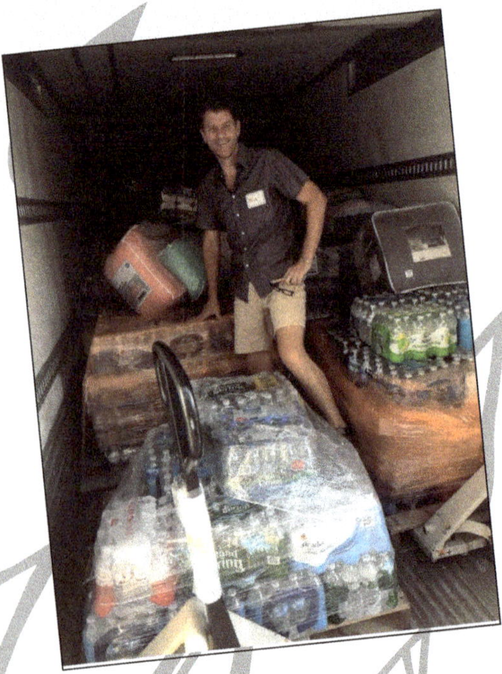

HARVEY
RELIEF HUB

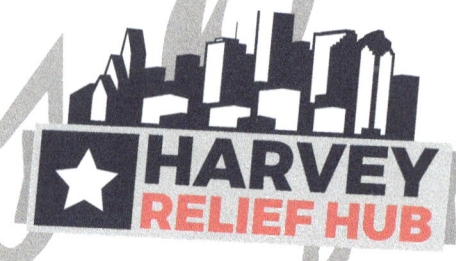

Starting the Hub **was not easy.** I didn't know what I was doing, and I had never done such a thing before. It was met with resistance and doubt.

But we kept going and just did it.

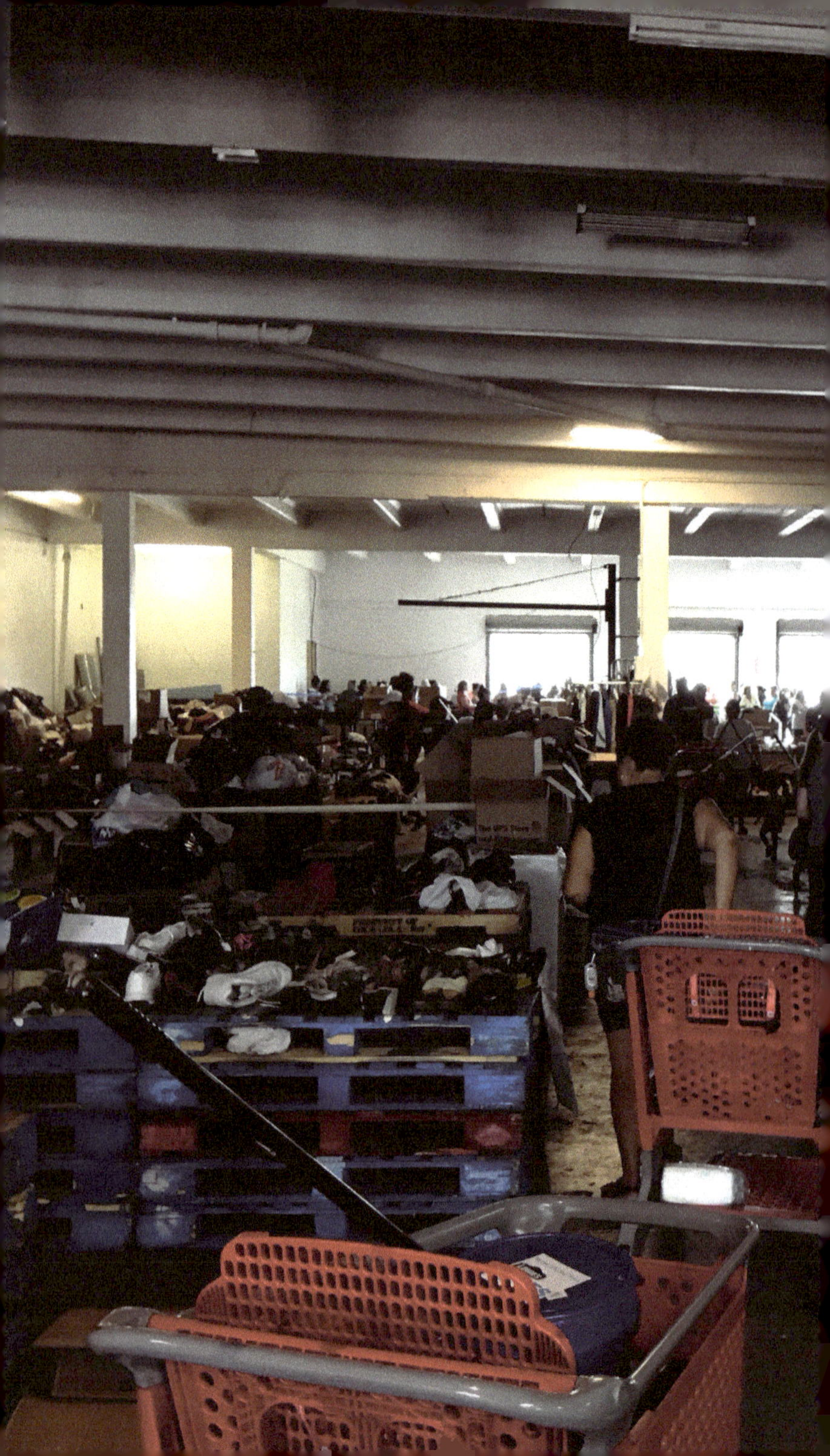

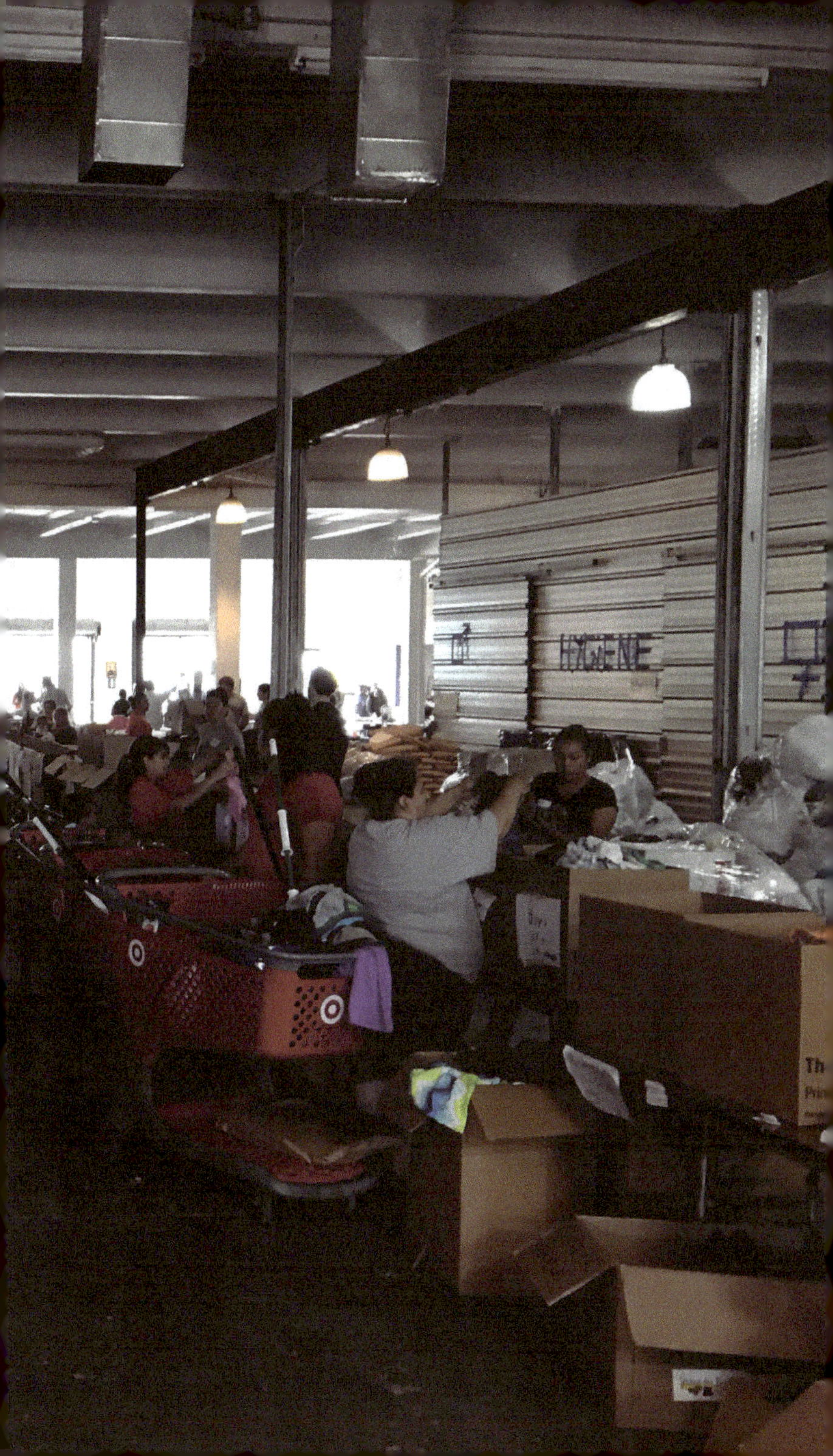

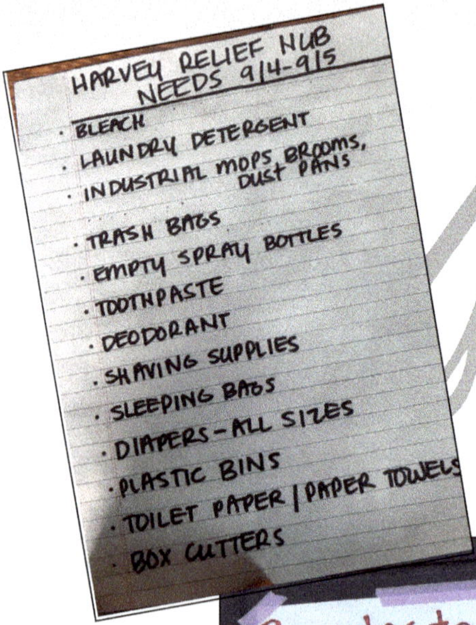
HARVEY RELIEF HUB
NEEDS 9/4-9/5
· BLEACH
· LAUNDRY DETERGENT
· INDUSTRIAL MOPS, BROOMS, DUST PANS
· TRASH BAGS
· EMPTY SPRAY BOTTLES
· TOOTHPASTE
· DEODORANT
· SHAVING SUPPLIES
· SLEEPING BAGS
· DIAPERS - ALL SIZES
· PLASTIC BINS
· TOILET PAPER / PAPER TOWELS
· BOX CUTTERS

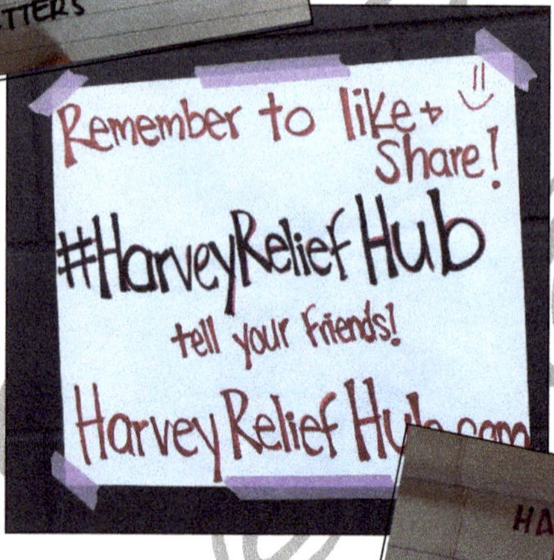
Remember to like + Share!
#HarveyReliefHub
tell your friends!
HarveyReliefHub.com

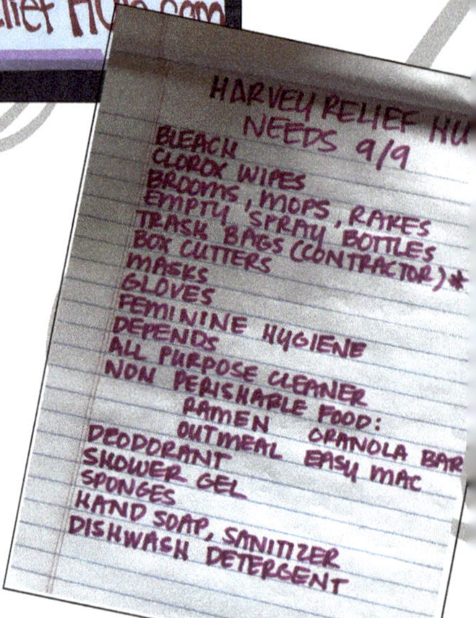
HARVEY RELIEF HU
NEEDS 9/9
BLEACH
CLOROX WIPES
BROOMS, MOPS, RAKES
EMPTY SPRAY BOTTLES
TRASH BAGS (CONTRACTOR)*
BOX CUTTERS
MASKS
GLOVES
FEMININE HYGIENE
DEPENDS
ALL PURPOSE CLEANER
NON PERISHABLE FOOD:
RAMEN GRANOLA BAR
OATMEAL EASY MAC
DEODORANT
SHOWER GEL
SPONGES
HAND SOAP, SANITIZER
DISHWASH DETERGENT

We received donations and volunteers almost exclusively through posts on Facebook, Next Door, and, really, through word of mouth.

On a typical daily basis, we would receive a warehouse full of donations and then proceed to give it all away. EVERY DAY. Never knowing for sure from where or when the next donation would come. It really was a <u>leap of faith</u> and held together by a <u>belief in the goodness of people</u>. It was astounding to me to see all of those who were willing to donate and serve others out of a warehouse without air conditioning or basic comforts.

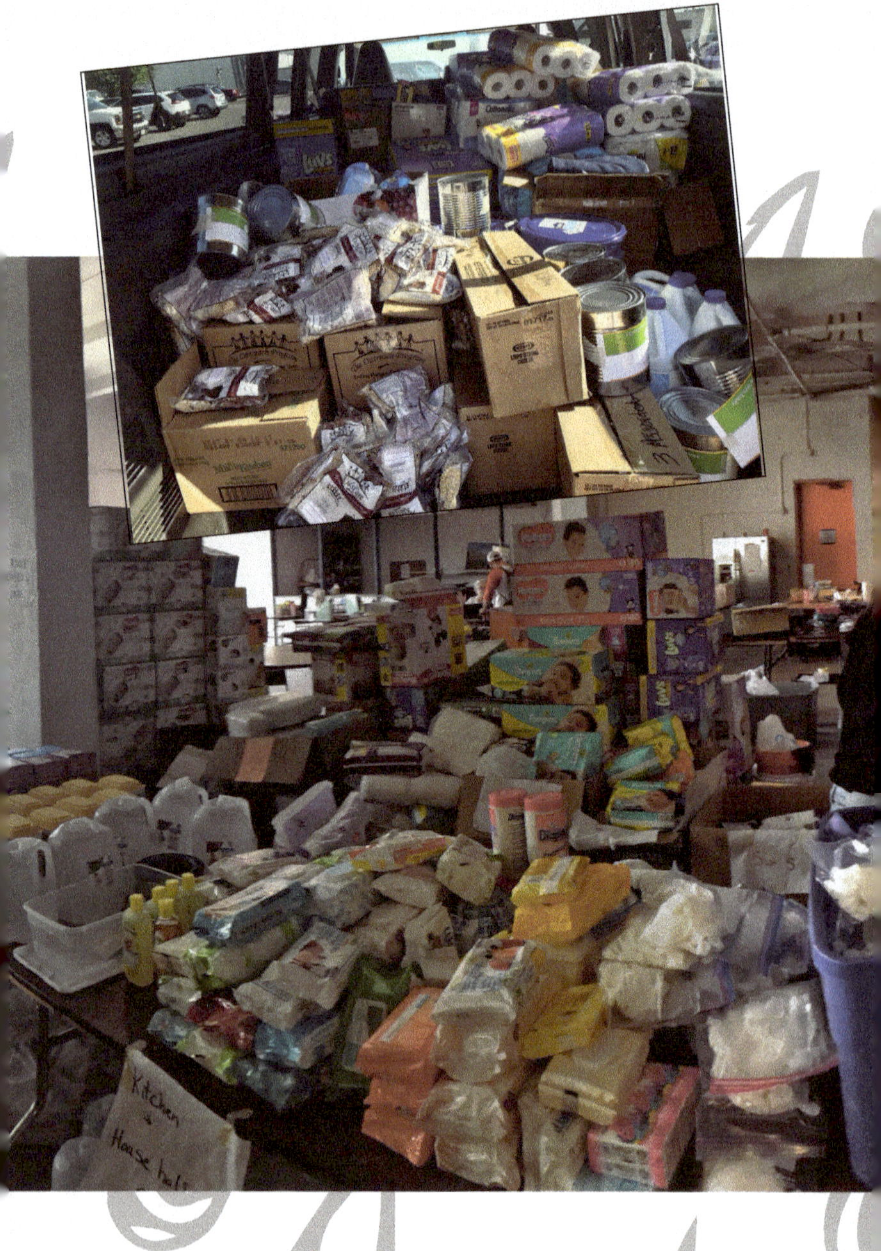
Kitchen

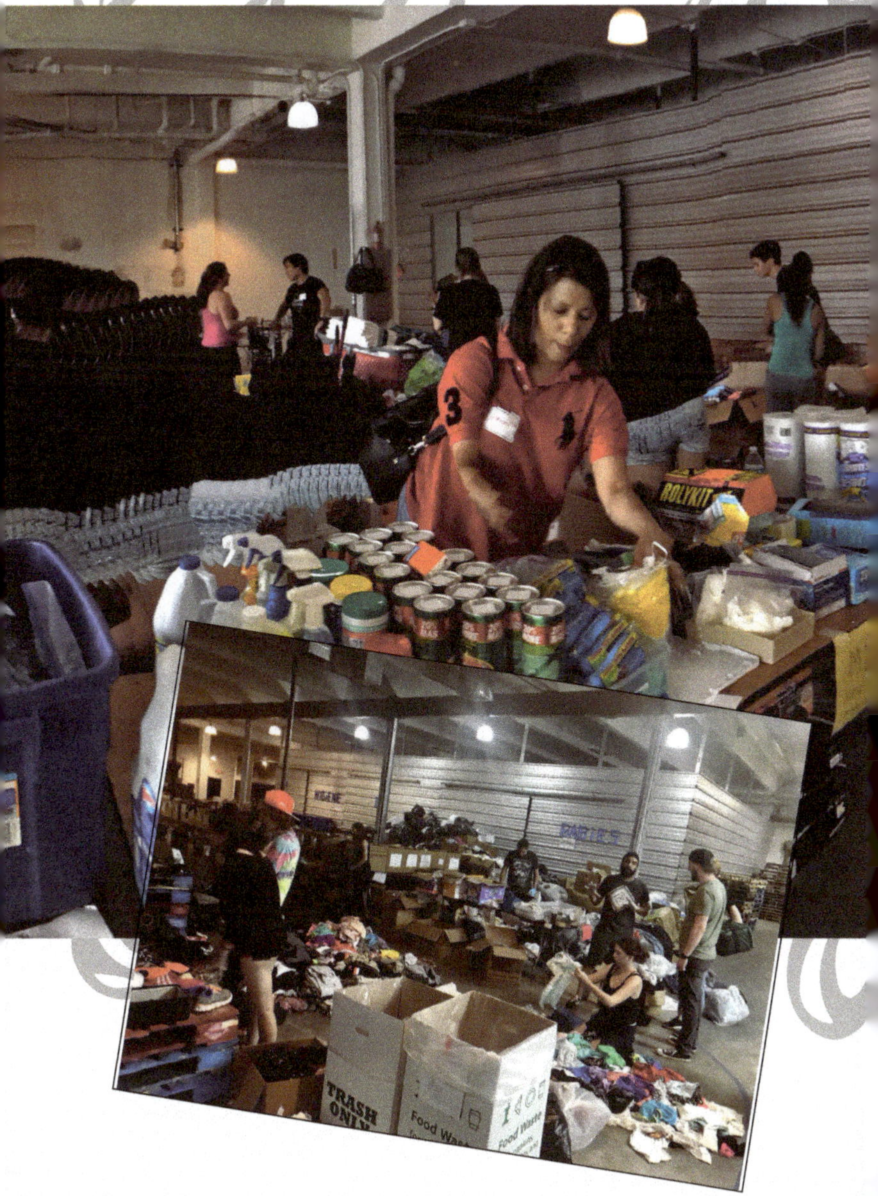
ROLYKIT
BABIES
TRASH ONLY

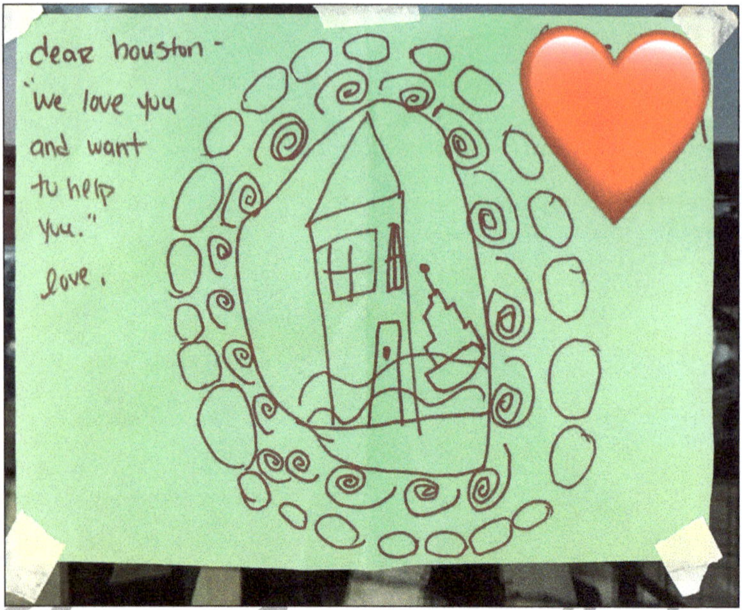
dear houston -
"we love you
and want
to help
you."
love,

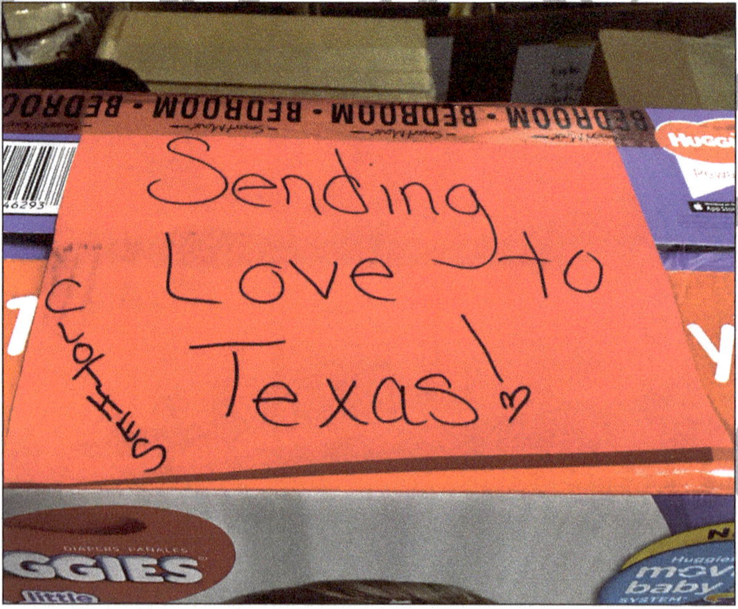
Sending
Love to
Texas!

After the storm, countless caring people brought much needed items from almost every state in the country: Boy Scout Troops, businesses of every type, families, church groups. Literally thousands came by car, van, suburban, and 18 wheeler with donations and a helping heart.

And at the same time each day, usually hours before we opened, individuals, families and children would line up to receive items that they or others they knew needed. It would break your heart to see the tremendous needs of those in line each day. That is what kept us inspired to do more, to not stop, and to find additional ways to help even more others in need. To those seeking assistance, we asked no questions. It became: just take what is needed and share with others in need.

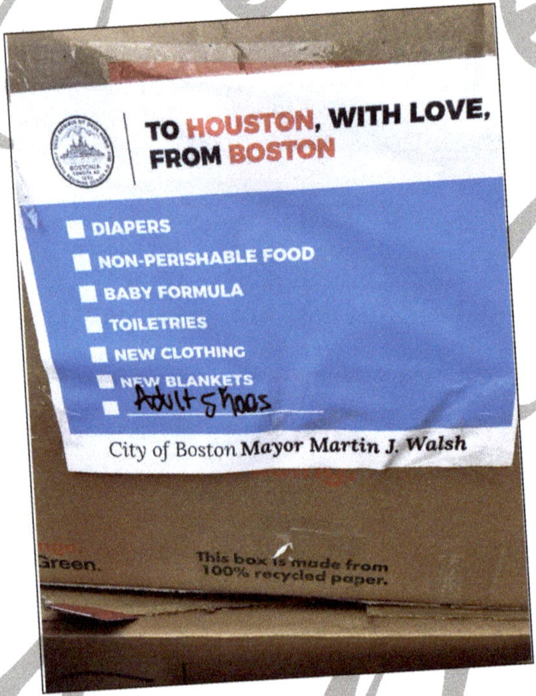
TO HOUSTON, WITH LOVE,
FROM BOSTON
DIAPERS
NON-PERISHABLE FOOD
BABY FORMULA
TOILETRIES
NEW CLOTHING
NEW BLANKETS
Adult Shoes
City of Boston Mayor Martin J. Walsh
This box is made from
100% recycled paper.

The Harvey Relief Hub was just one of hundreds, if not thousands, of loosely organized, volunteer-led groups that gathered together to serve. Through that experience, I truly saw the good in people—in our city, our state, and across the nation. The <u>outpouring of support restored my faith in humanity</u> in an age when we have all began to question our differences, which seem to be highlighted on a daily basis.

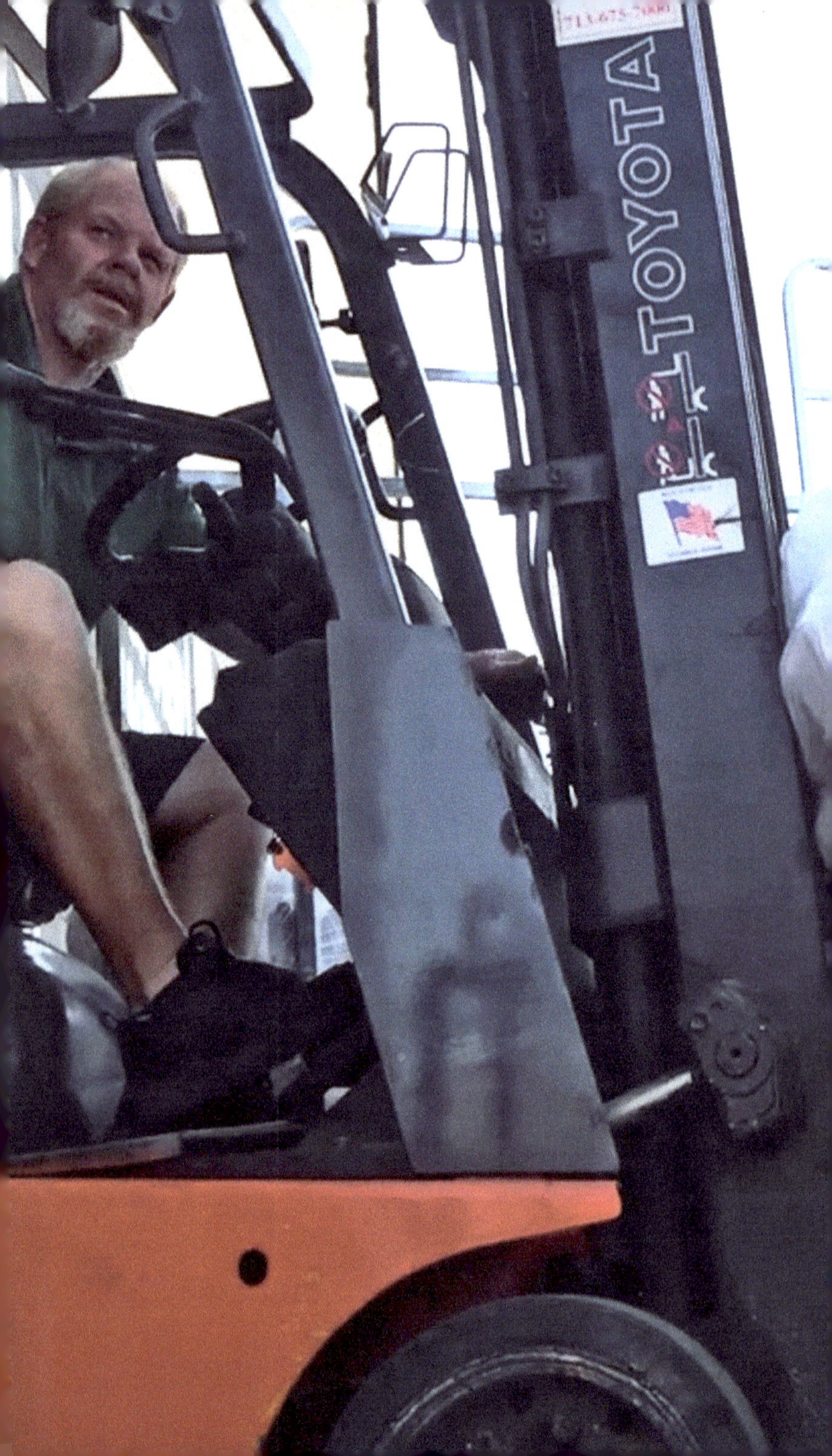
TOYOTA

It is still hard to describe, yet heartwarming to think about, the countless Harvey Heroes who stepped up to serve those in need. Of course we were in awe of true heroes: the police and firefighters, our public servants, men and women who risked their lives to save others. But just as important were the everyday heroes who rose to the occasion to serve when needed most. Cooking food for strangers, rescuing neighbors, mucking out homes, caring for animals. There were thousands out there. Distributing medicine. Food. Cleaning supplies.

For 112 days, I worked almost exclusively in Harvey Recovery. I was fortunate to have amazing friends, employees, and clients who supported these efforts and understood both the need and my desire to help others.

Over time, the City of Houston ended up merging their own relief operations into ours, and I am honored to have led the City of Houston's Puerto Rican Relief Effort Delegation, showing the world how appreciative we were for receiving aid and that we wanted to pay it forward in helping our neighbors and fellow countrymen.

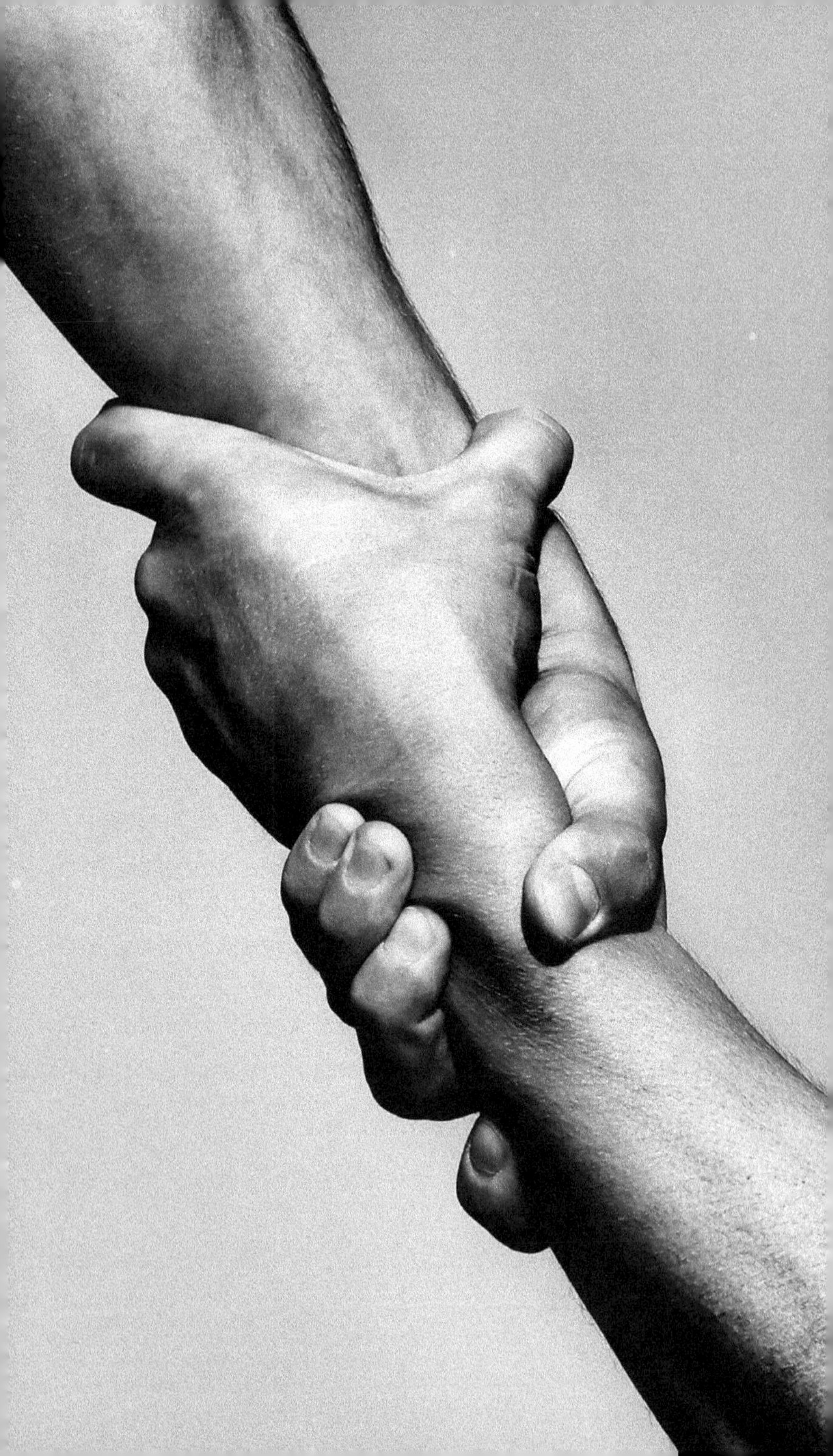

It is times like these that define a city and its people.

We are not the same today.

Nor should we be.

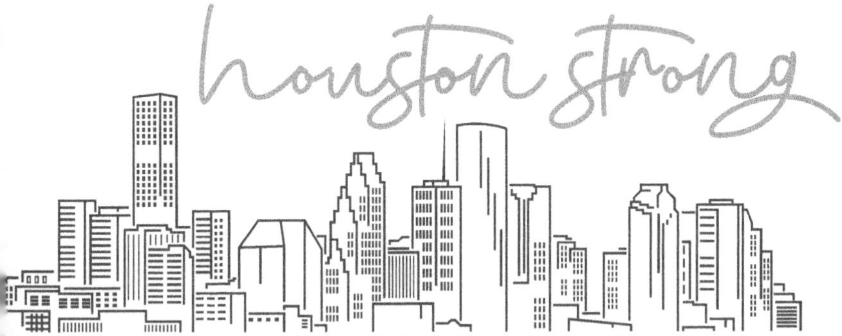
houston strong

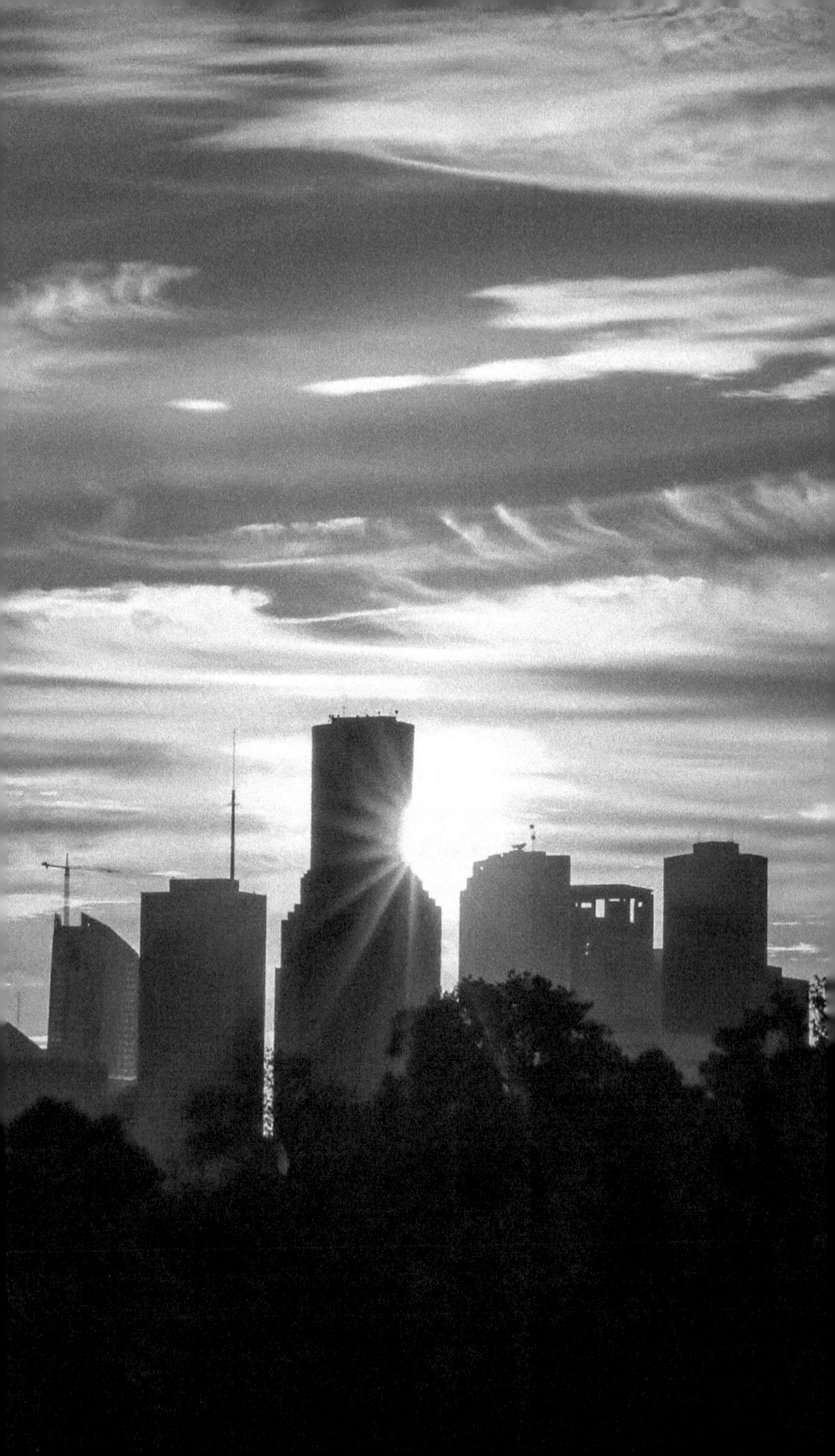

I hope, as you graduate today, you will not only reflect on the time you spent here. Just as importantly, reflect on what you will do with your time now, from this point forward.

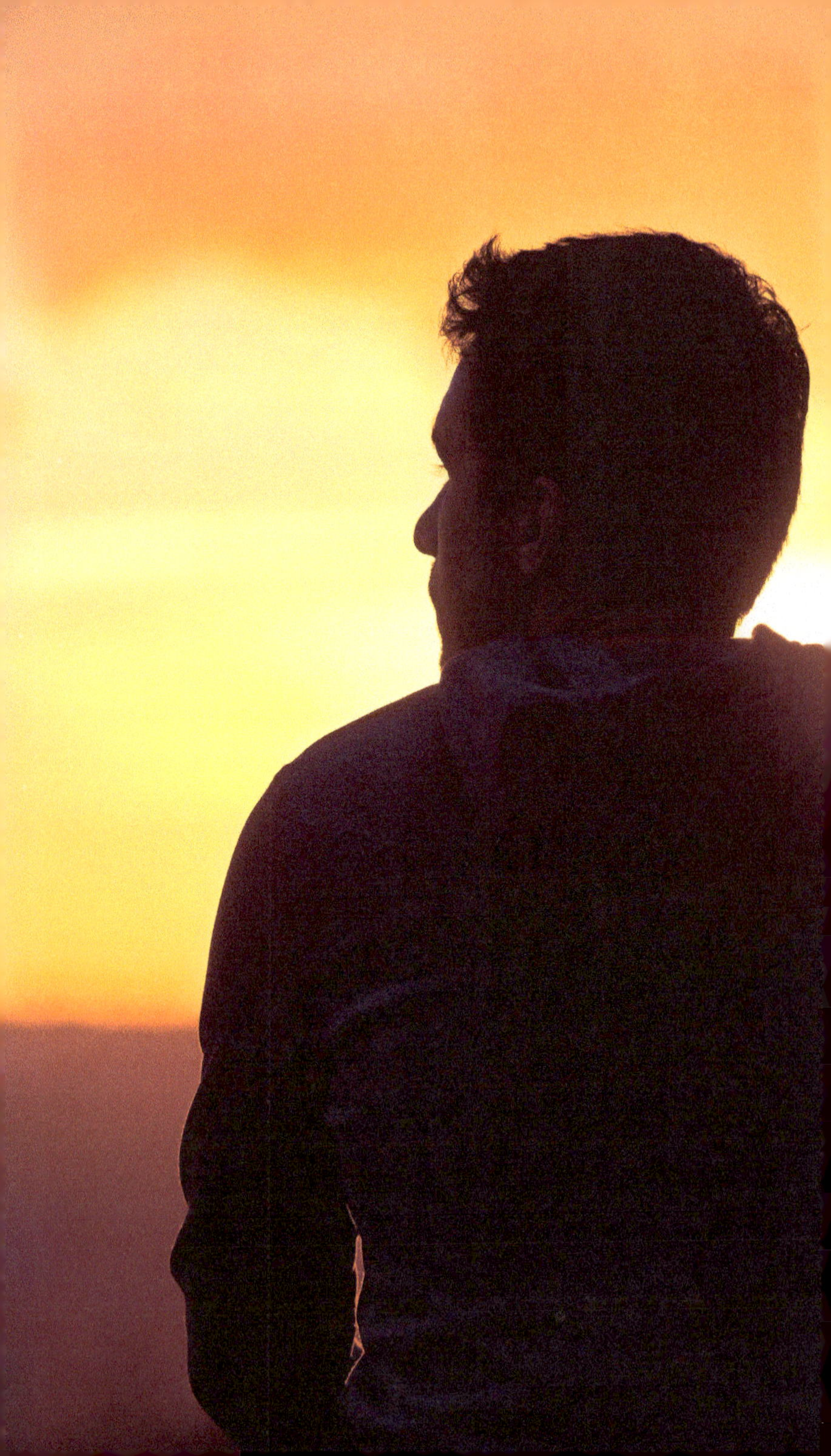

These are the lessons I learned from that life-changing experience:

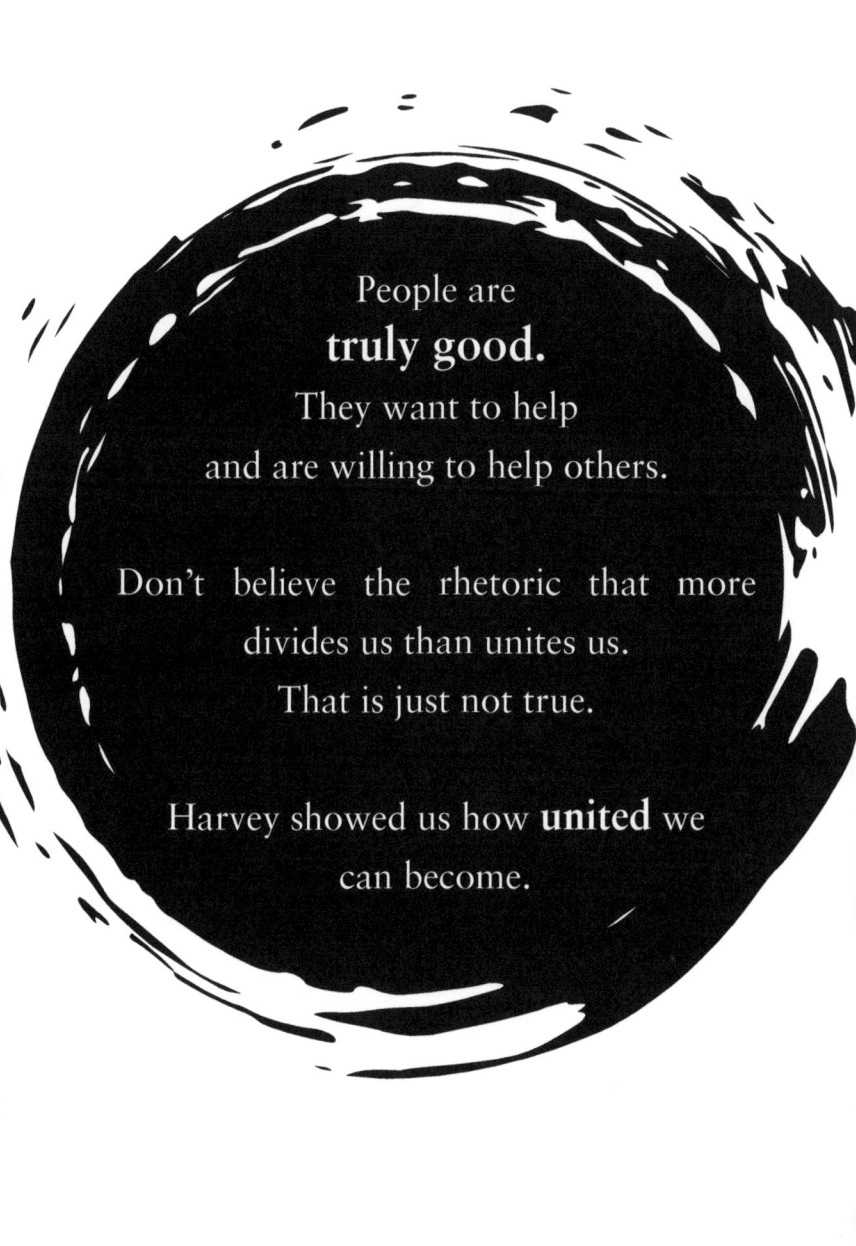

People are **truly good.** They want to help and are willing to help others.

Don't believe the rhetoric that more divides us than unites us. That is just not true.

Harvey showed us how **united** we can become.

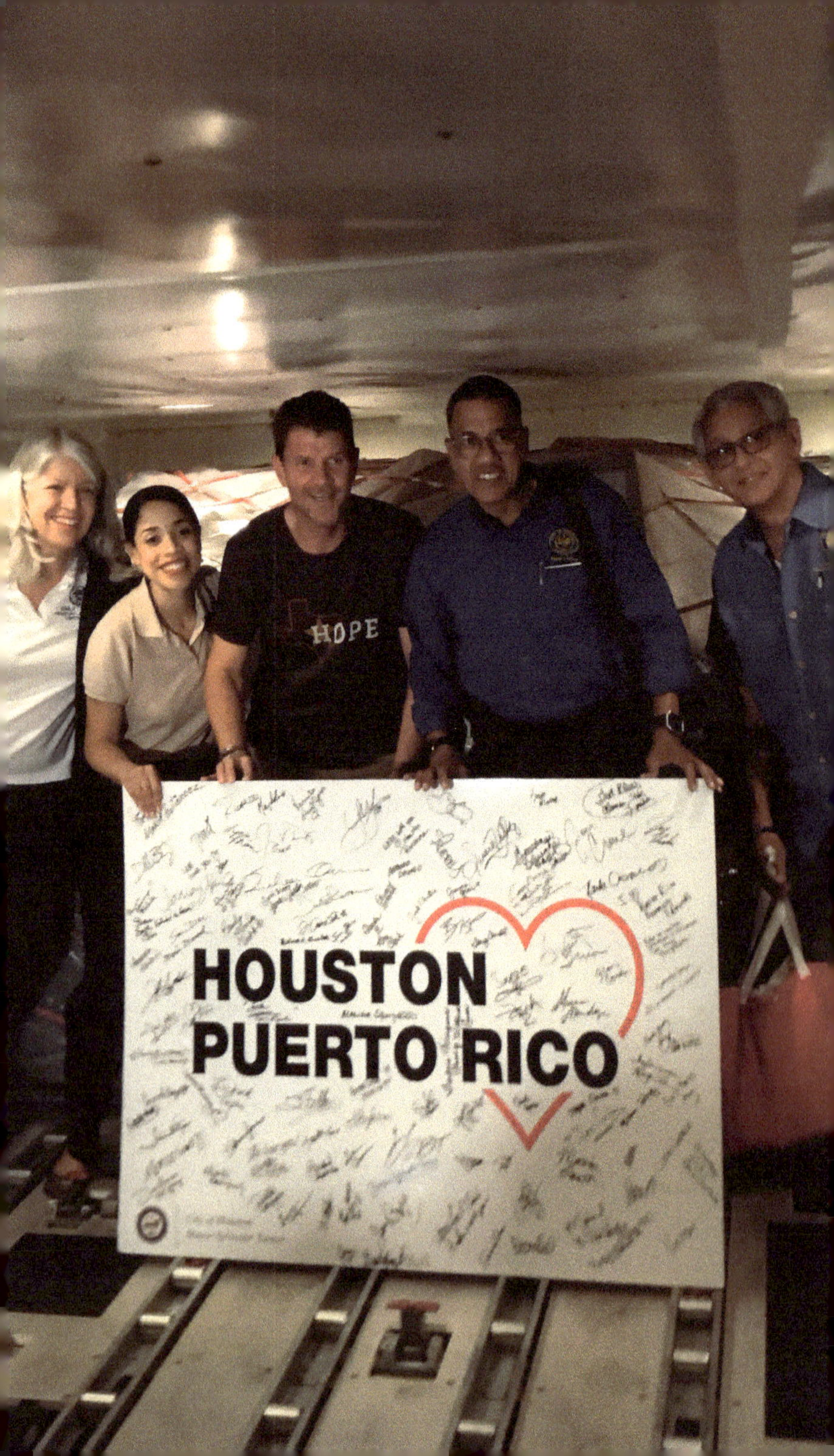
HOPE
HOUSTON
PUERTO RICO

Make no mistake.

**Good deeds require people
to take action.**

You must actually go and *do* good.

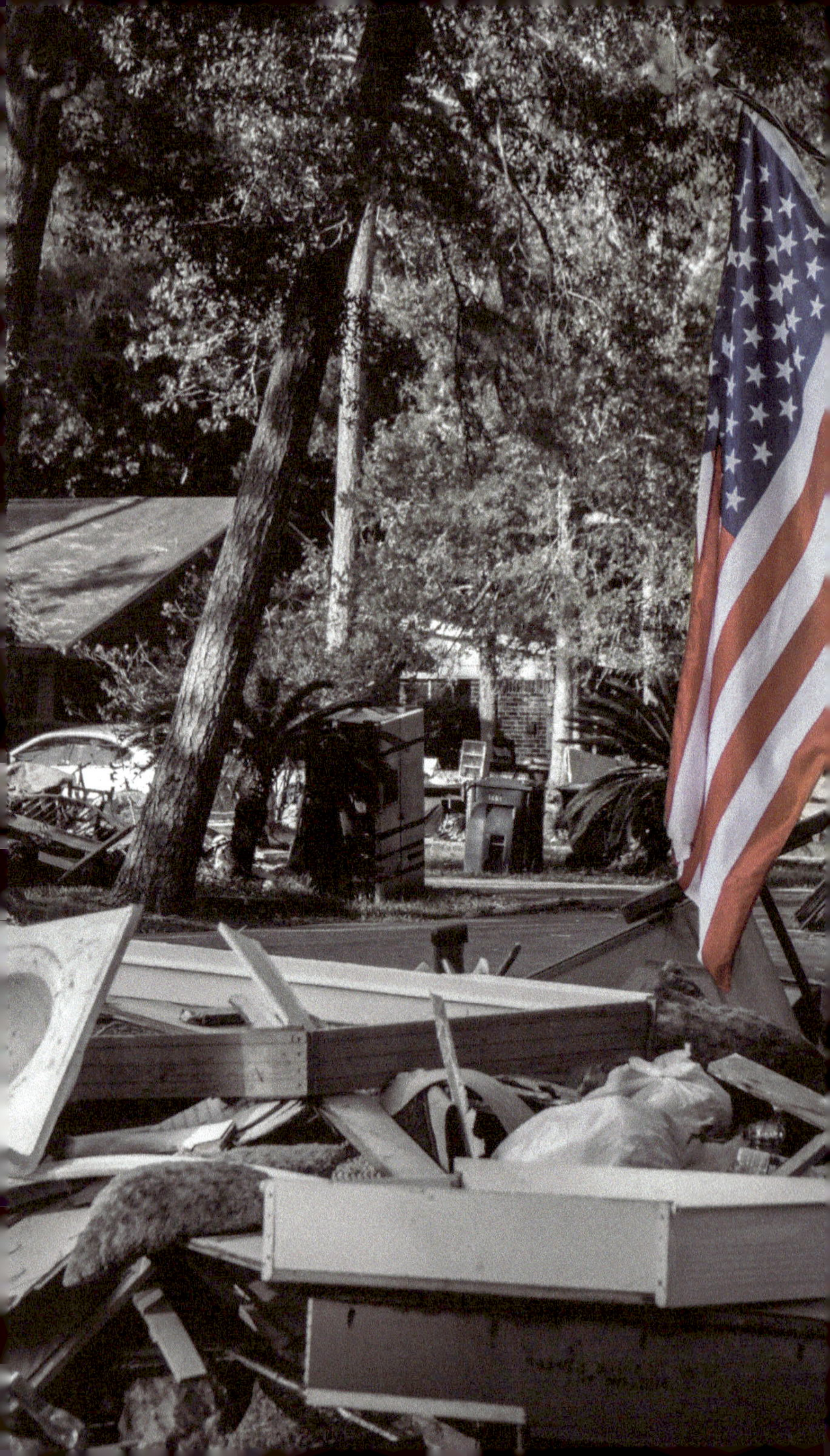

Seeing people arrive at the Hub with no hope, full of despair, I was reminded to look people in the eye—in their hearts, even—and to **treat everyone with respect.** After all, the hurricane flooded the homes of rich and poor, white and black, Democrat and Republican.

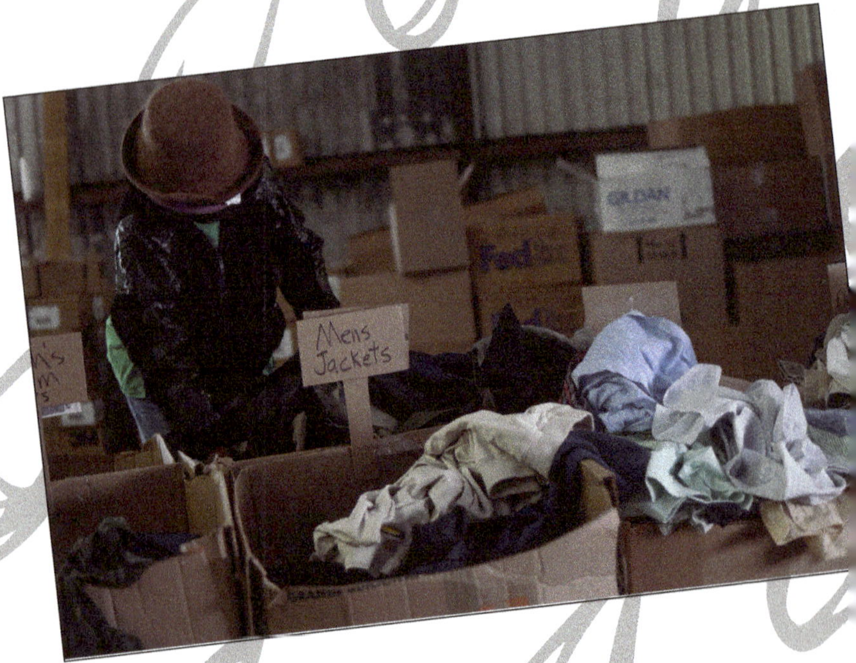
GILDAN
Mens Jackets

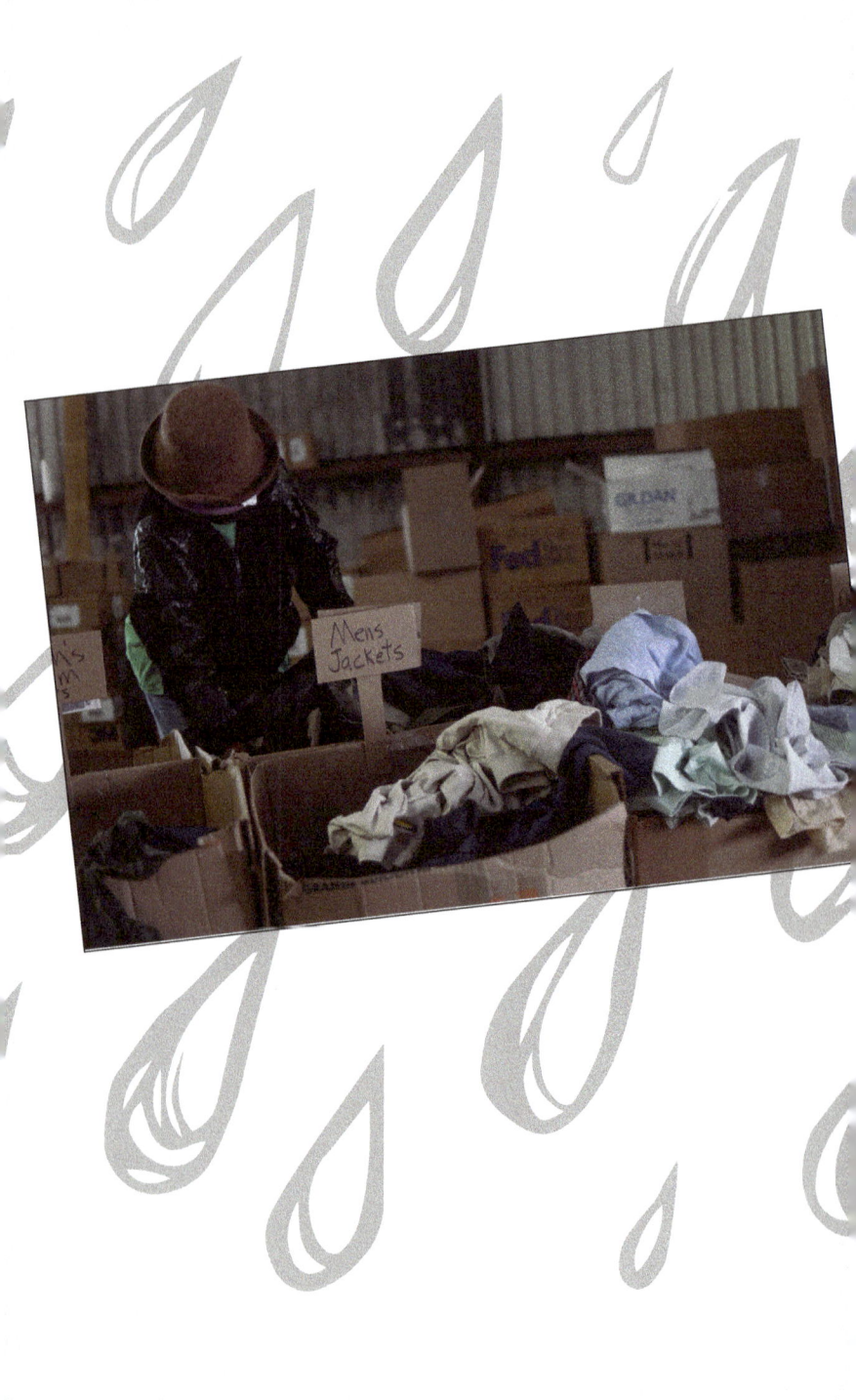

Harvey was a reminder that **we all need help at some point in our lives.**

So help others when you can, and you'll receive help graciously when you need it. Some needs are more apparent than others.

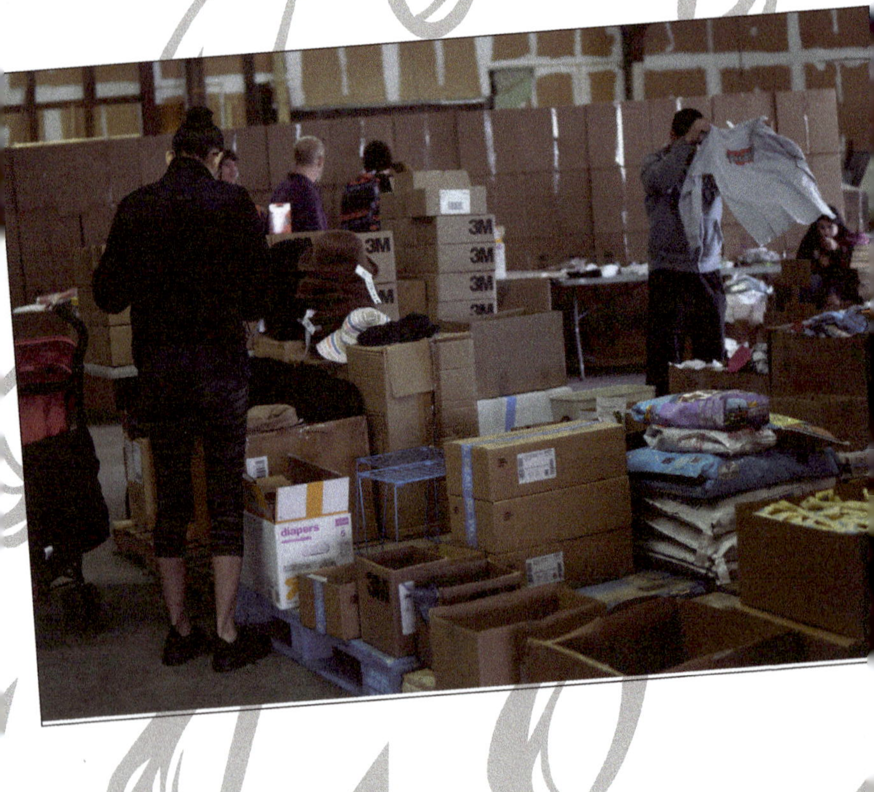
3M
diapers

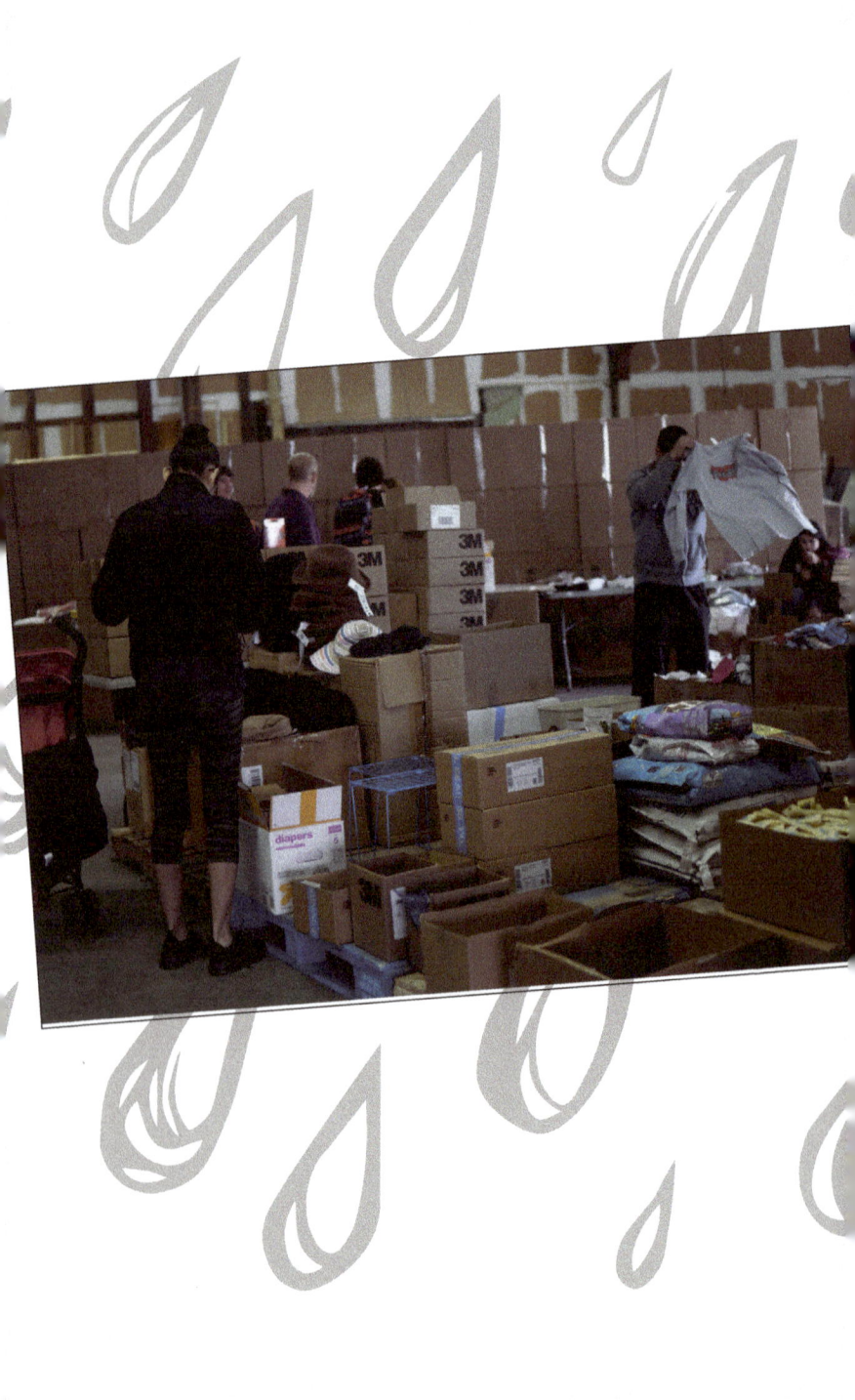

Just because things look one way, don't assume or believe all you see.

One snapshot or expose doesn't tell the whole story. It's important to see the complete picture.

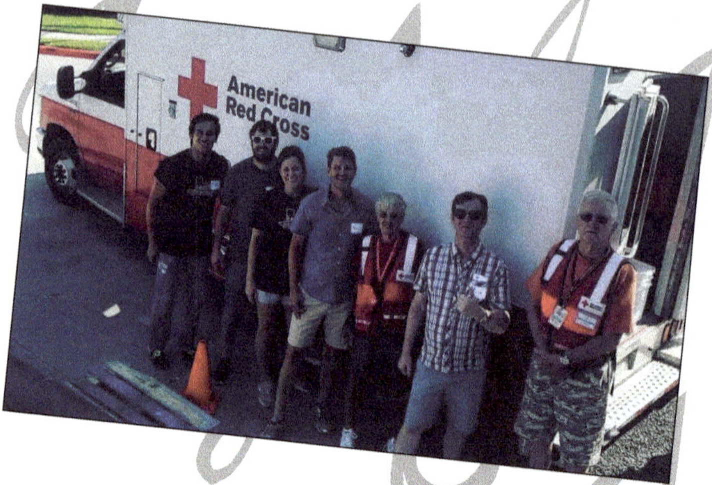
American
Red Cross

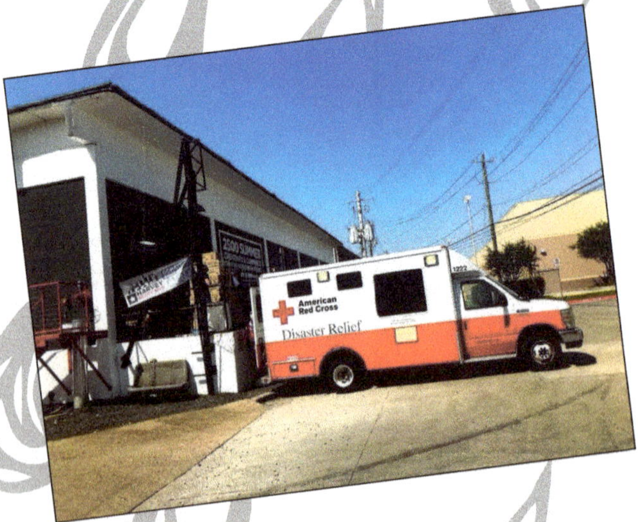
American
Red Cross
Disaster Relief

In the beginning we worked alongside the Red Cross. While I have great respect for organizations that are designed to help in disaster situations, I will always have a special place in my heart for the unorganized, entirely made up of those whose desire to help and ability to adapt quickly are the foundation of true service in our nation and around the world.

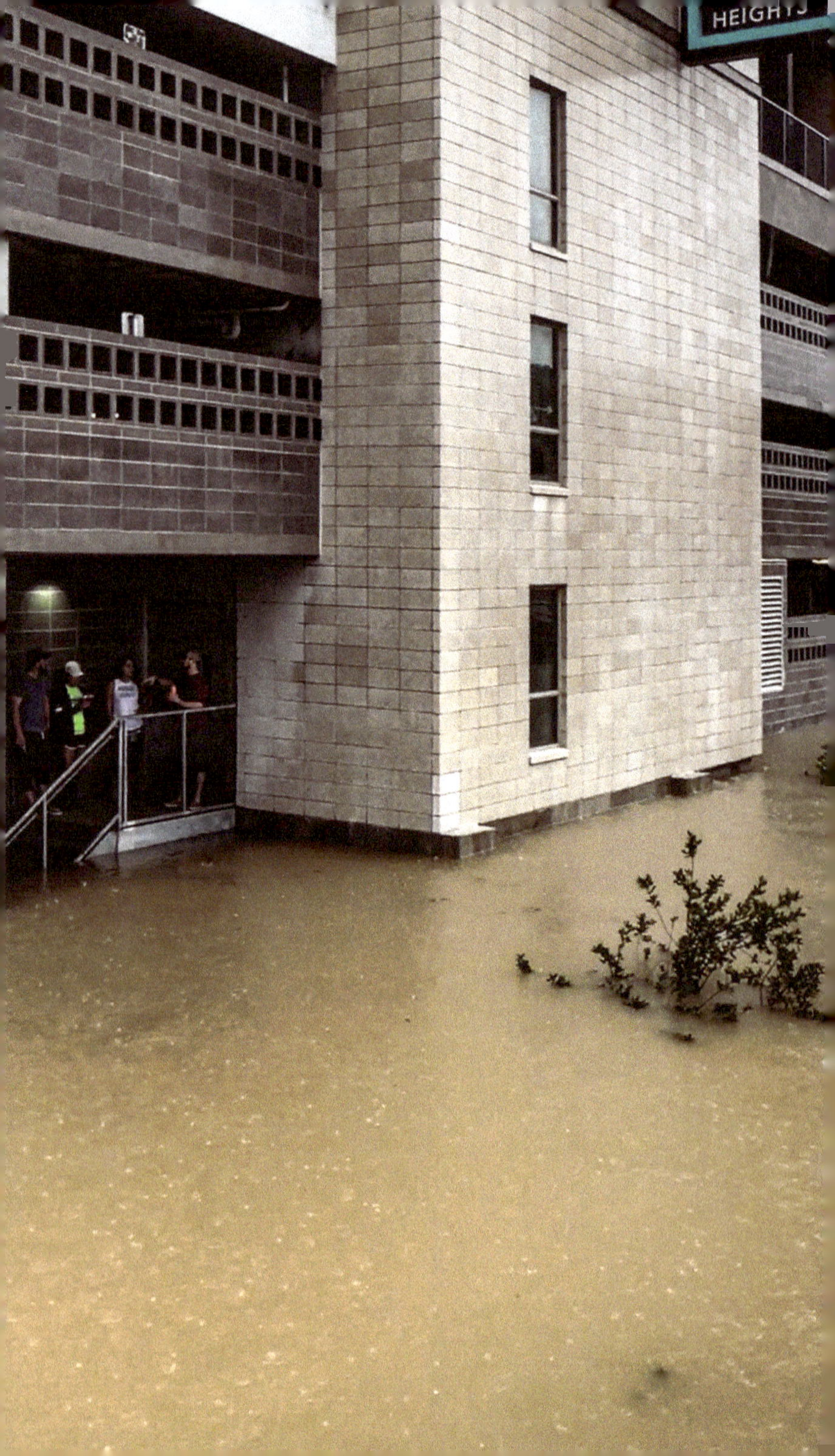
HEIGHTS

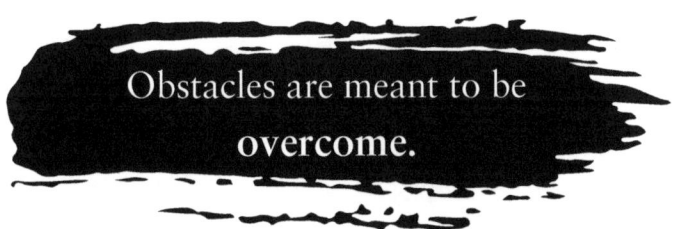

Obstacles are meant to be **overcome.**

Whether that is four feet of water on the way to serve or any other roadblock along the way.

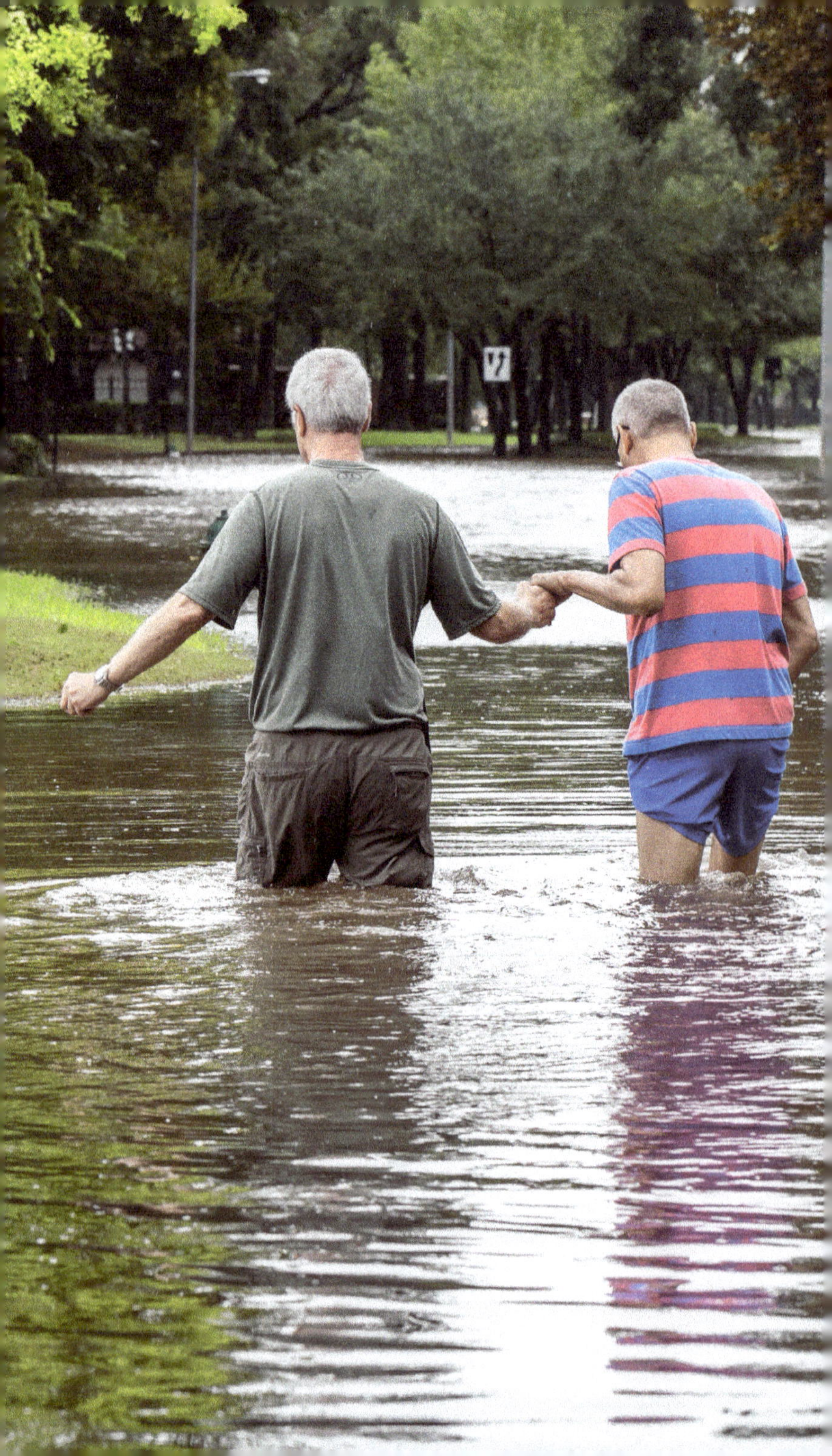

If it were easy, everyone would do it.
Do it *because* it's difficult.

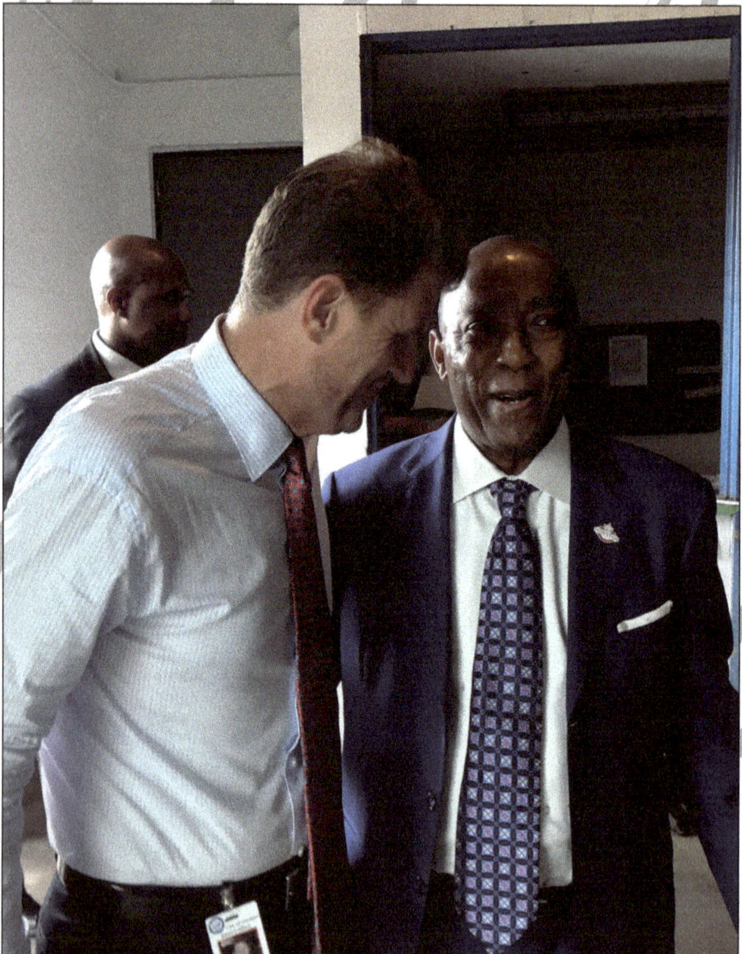

Don't expect the authorities to always say yes.

Follow your heart when you know it to be right, even if it is unpopular or misunderstood. History has taught us that rebels and non-conformists are often the ones to bring much-needed change to society.

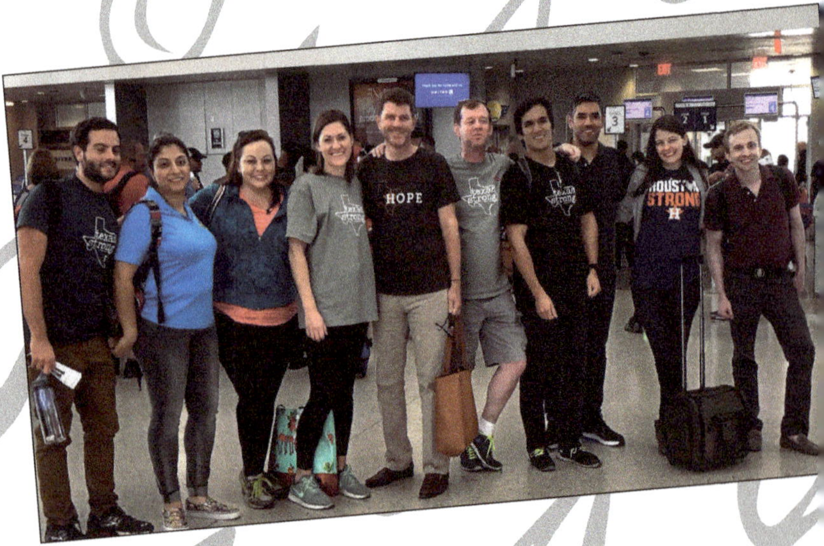
HOPE

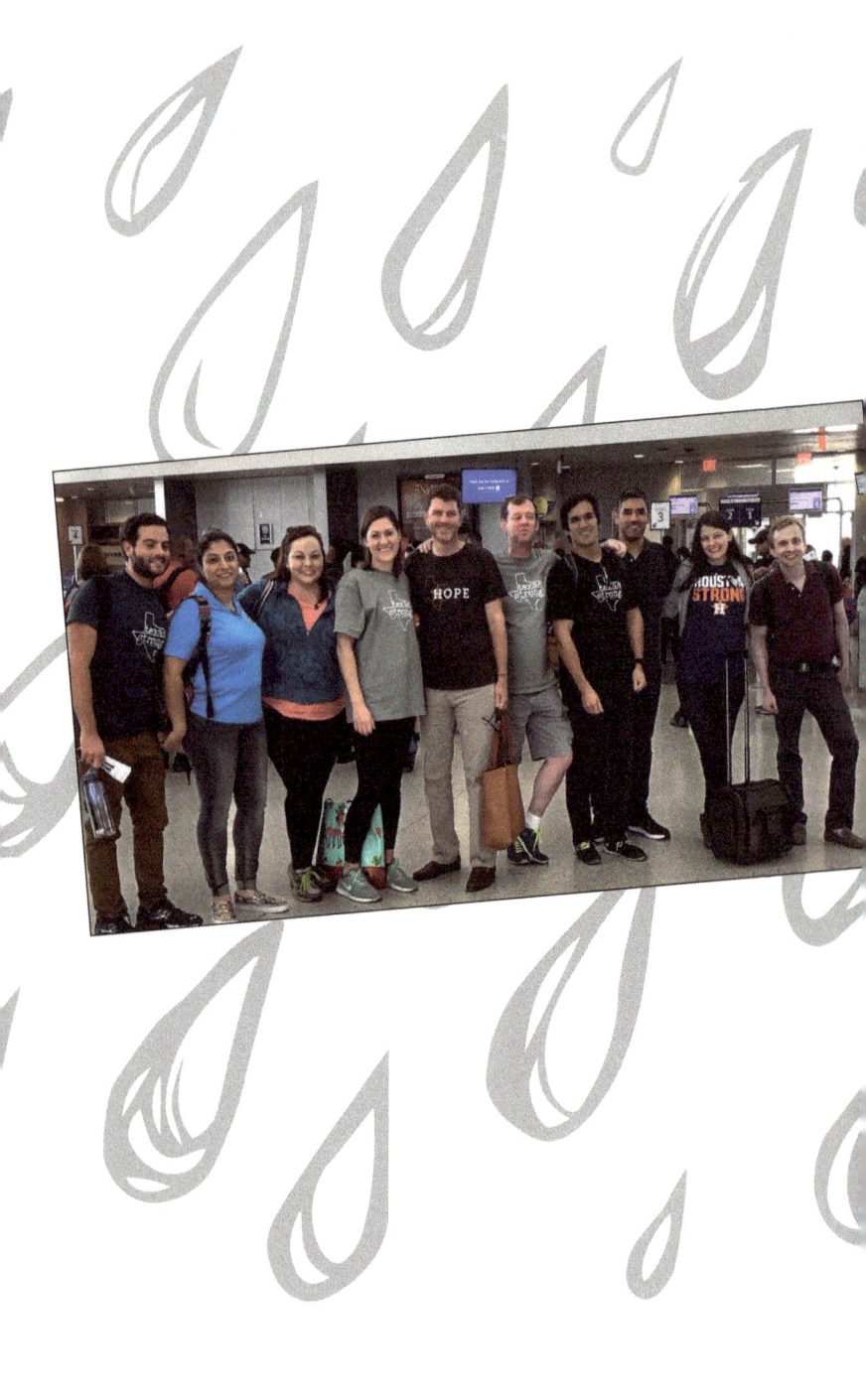

In life—to be successful—we must build **relationships** and **bridges**.
Not walls.

True lasting friendships go beyond political terms, semesters in college, and hurricane seasons.

Relationships matter.

Build realtionships whenever you can.

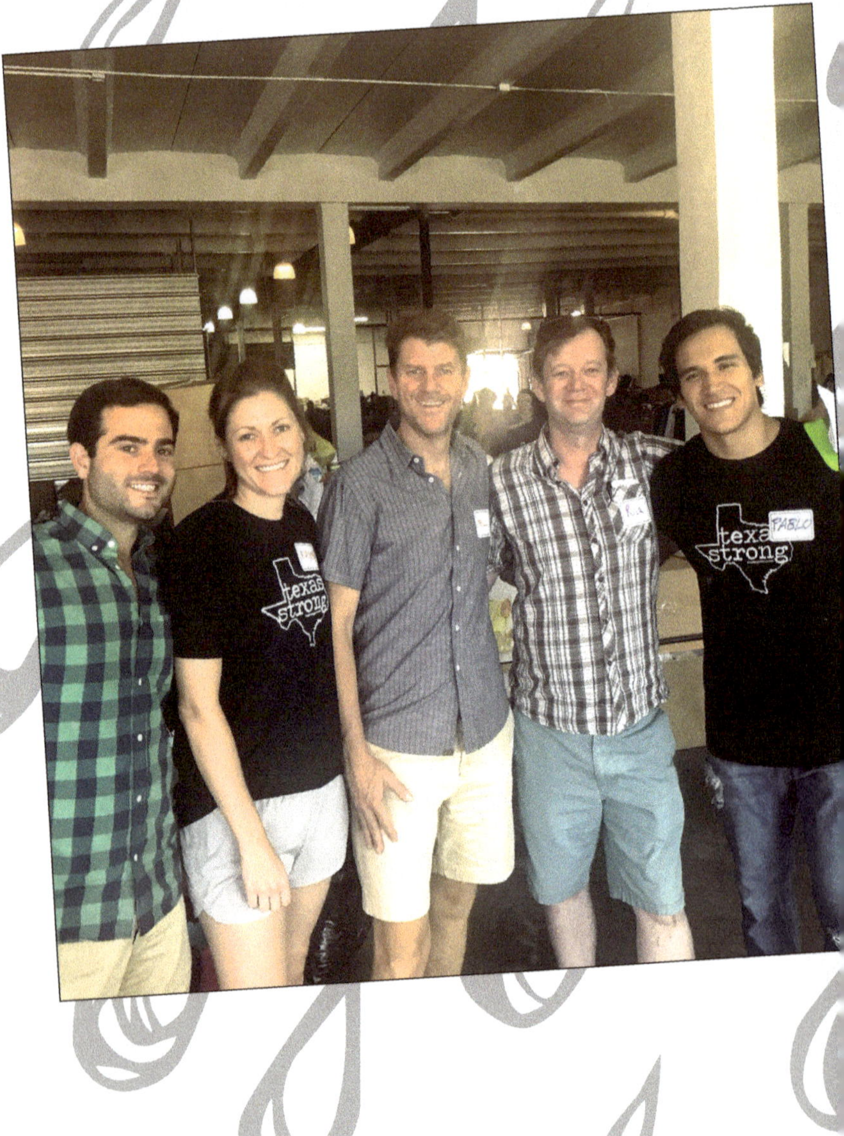
texas
strong
texas
strong
PABLO

Make friends.

Rely on friends.

Trust your friends;
they know you best.

Don't ever forget to
be a friend!

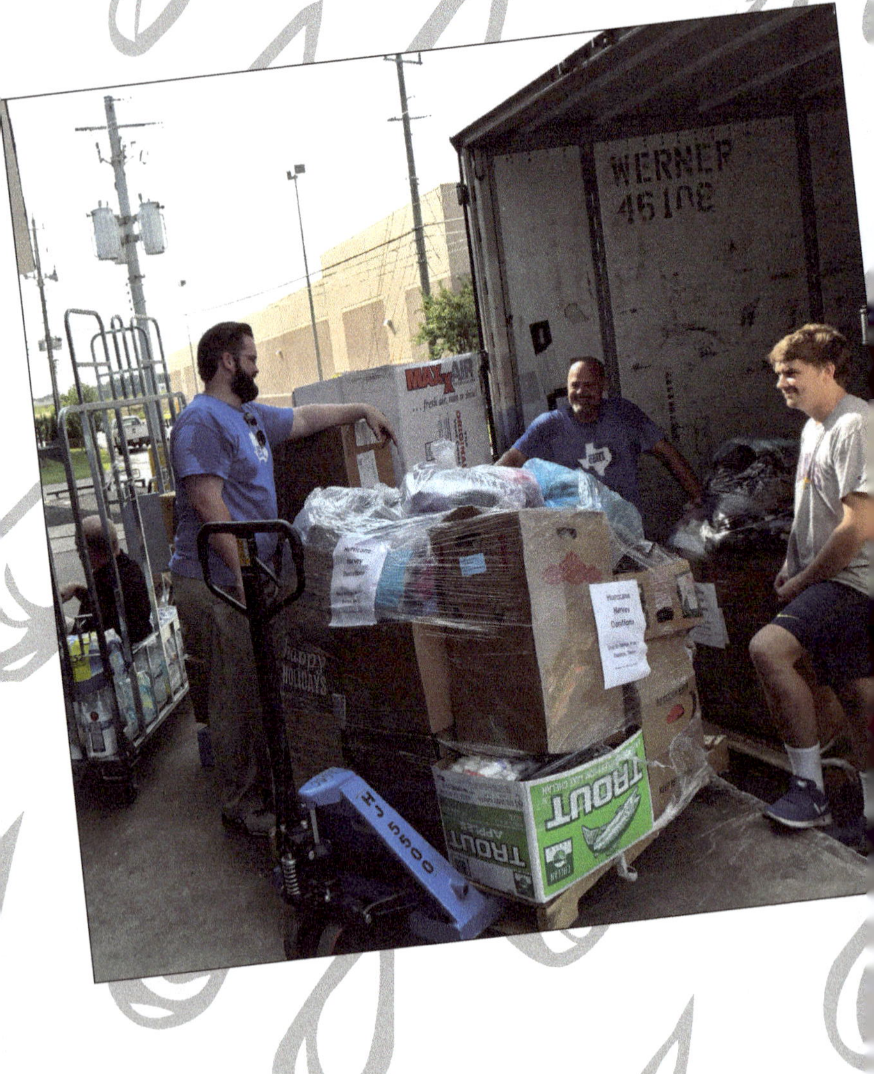
WERNER
MAX AIR
TROUT
APPLES
TROUT
Happy HOLIDAYS

We are stronger together.

We can do more **together**
than we can do by ourselves.

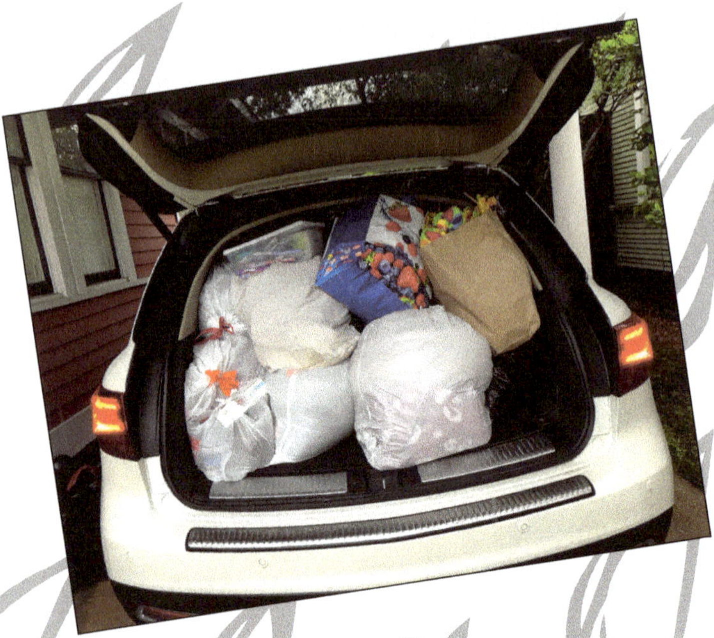

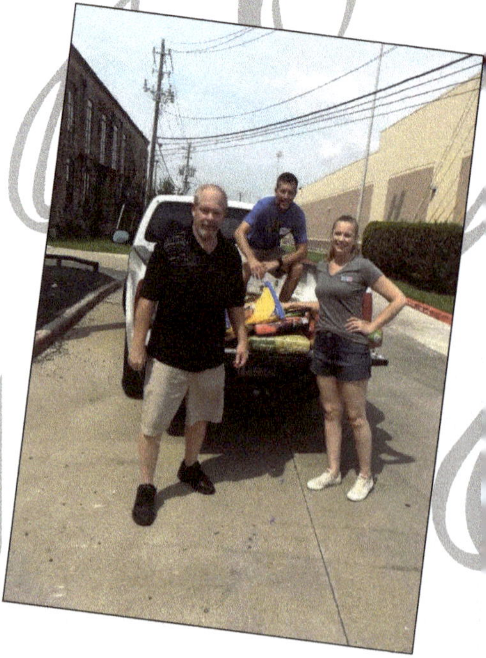

So give what you can.

Some of you have time.

Some of you have talent.

Some of you have treasure.

All are equally important.

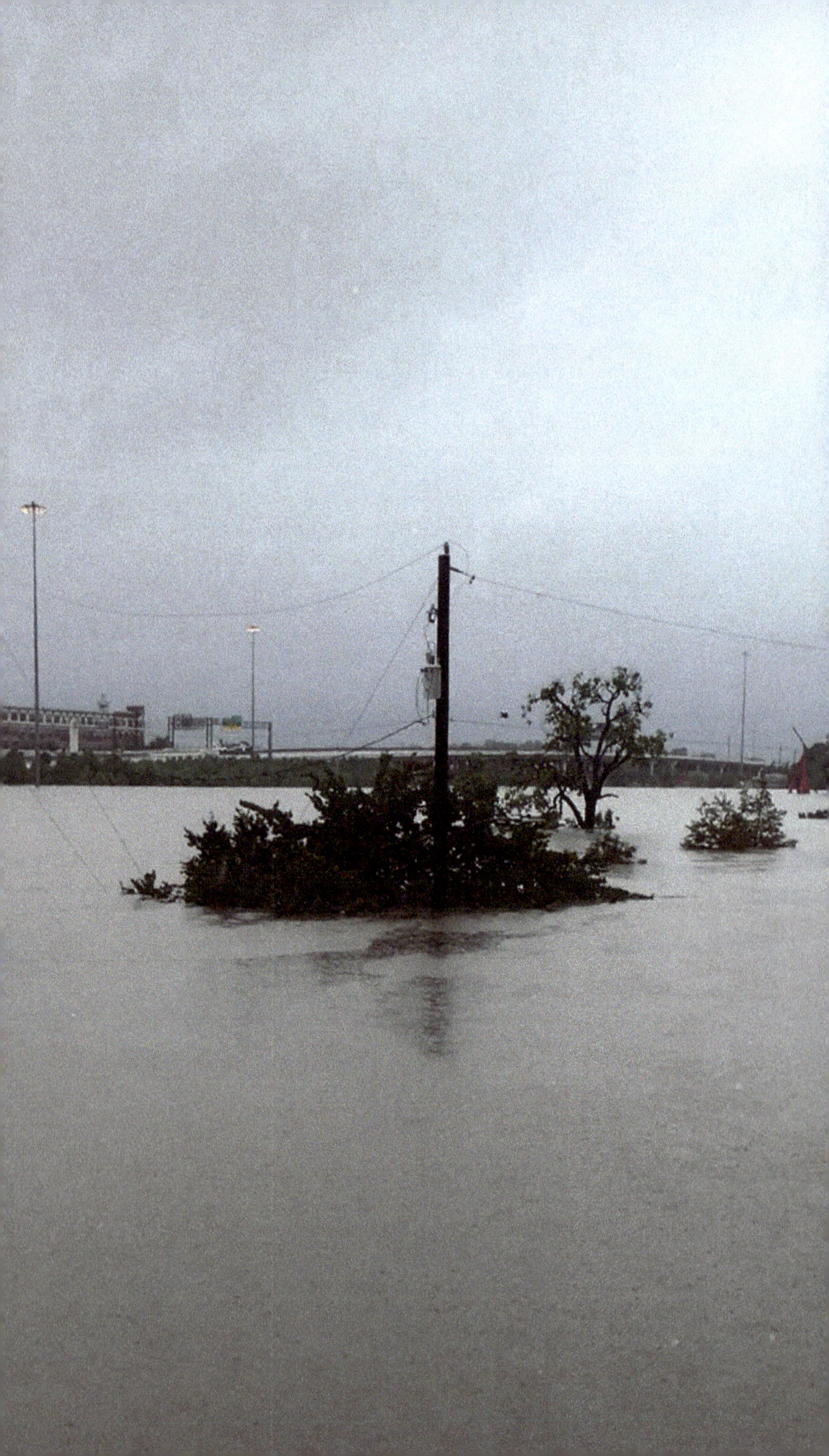

Hurricane seasons come and go.
Prepare for, and expect,
the unexpected.
Things happen.

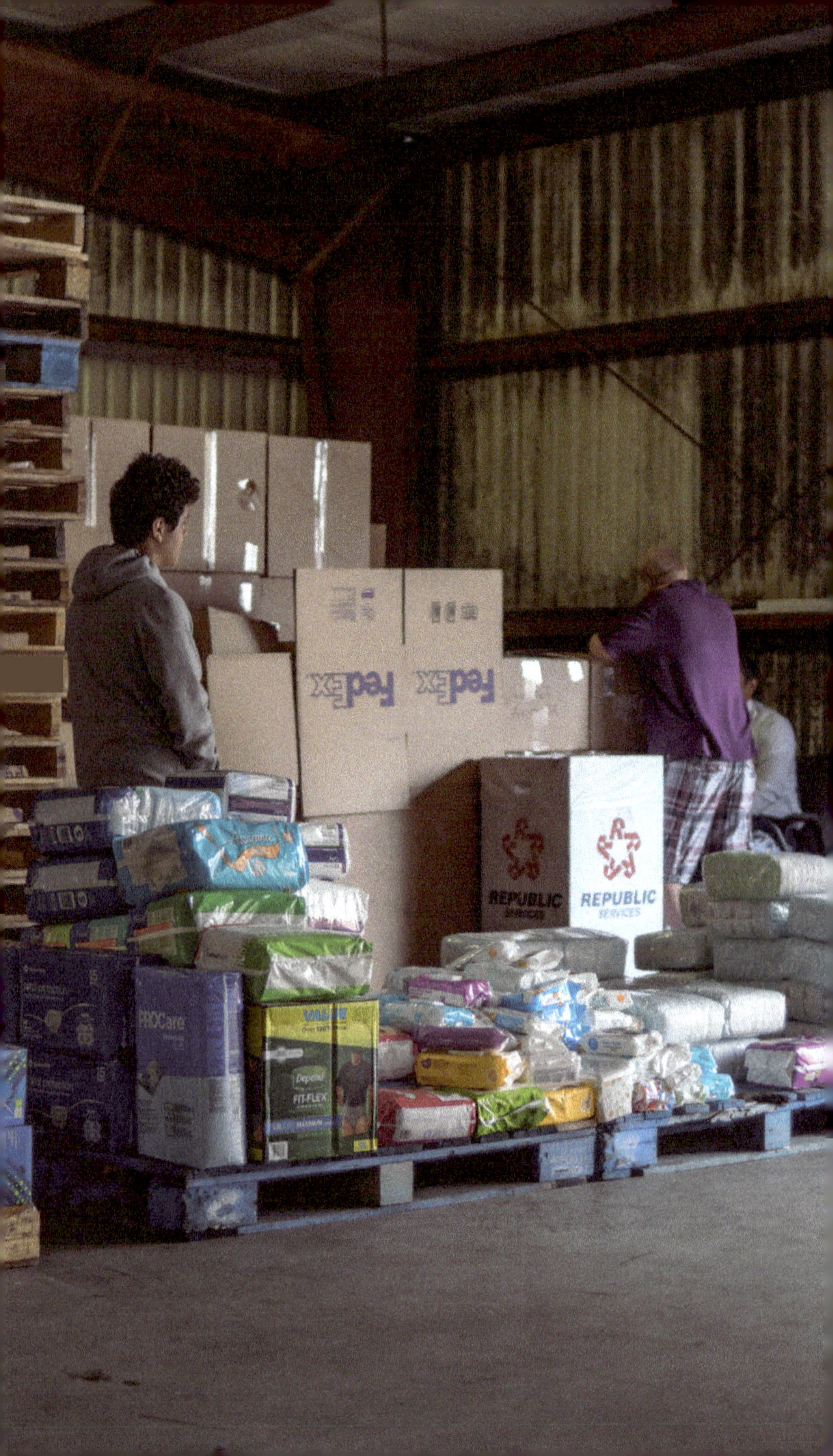
REPUBLIC
REPUBLIC
SERVICES
ProCare
VALUE
Depend
FIT-FLEX

It is often said that it is what we do that defines us.

More often, I believe, **it is what we *don't* do that haunts us for the rest of our lives.**

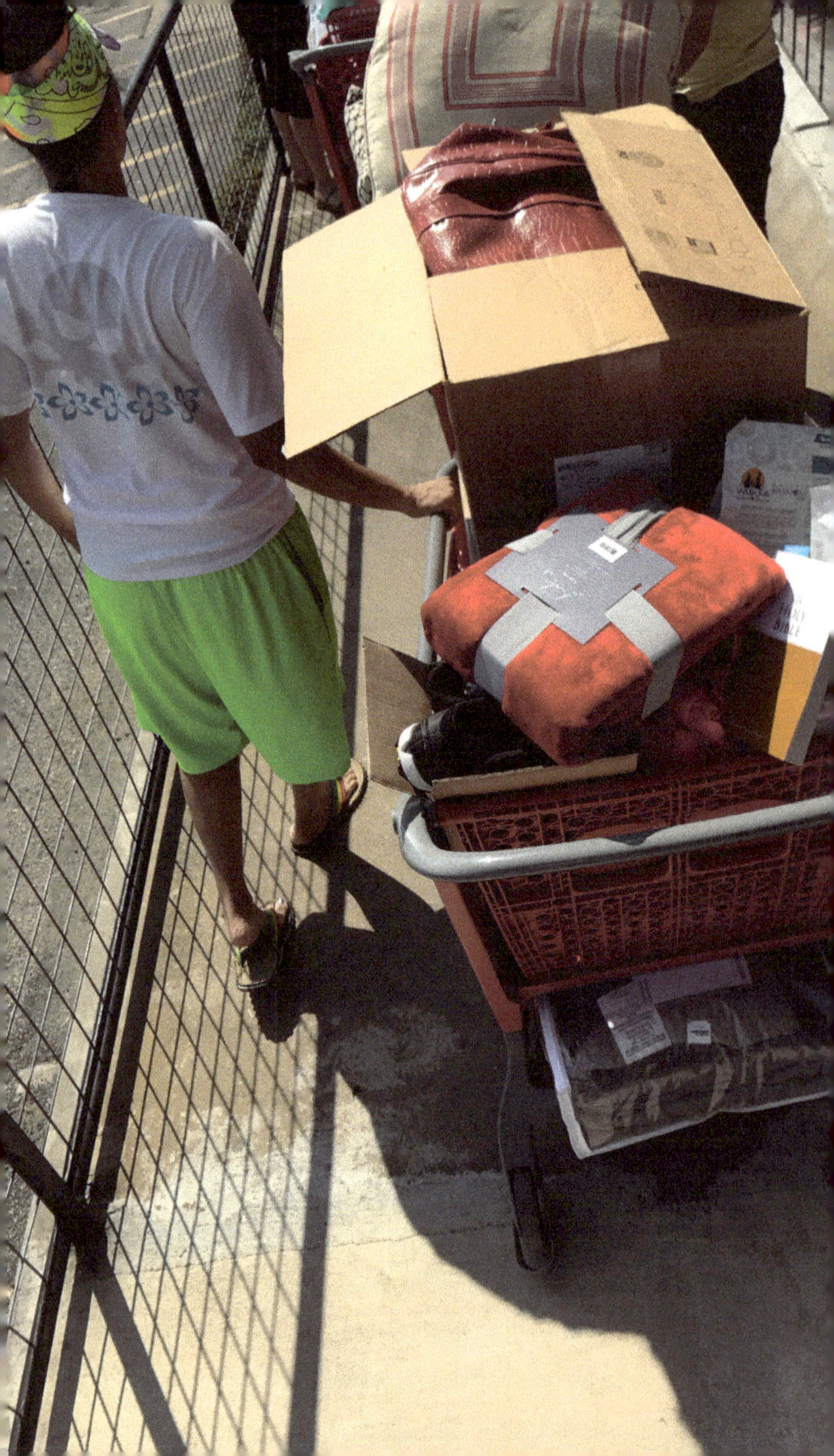

Don't lose
an opportunity
when you have it.

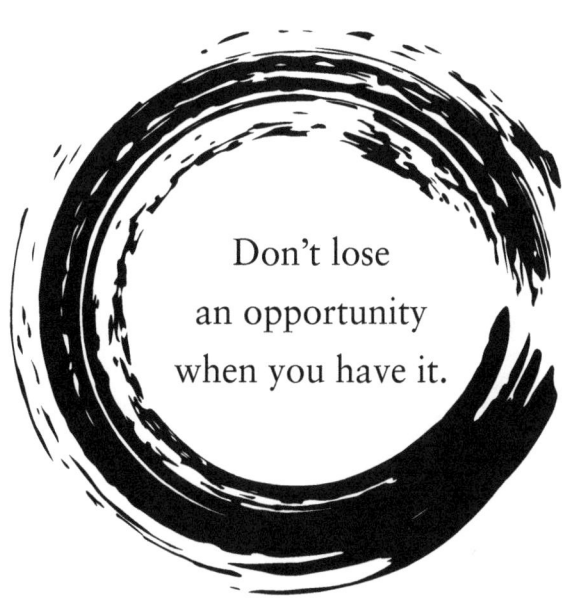

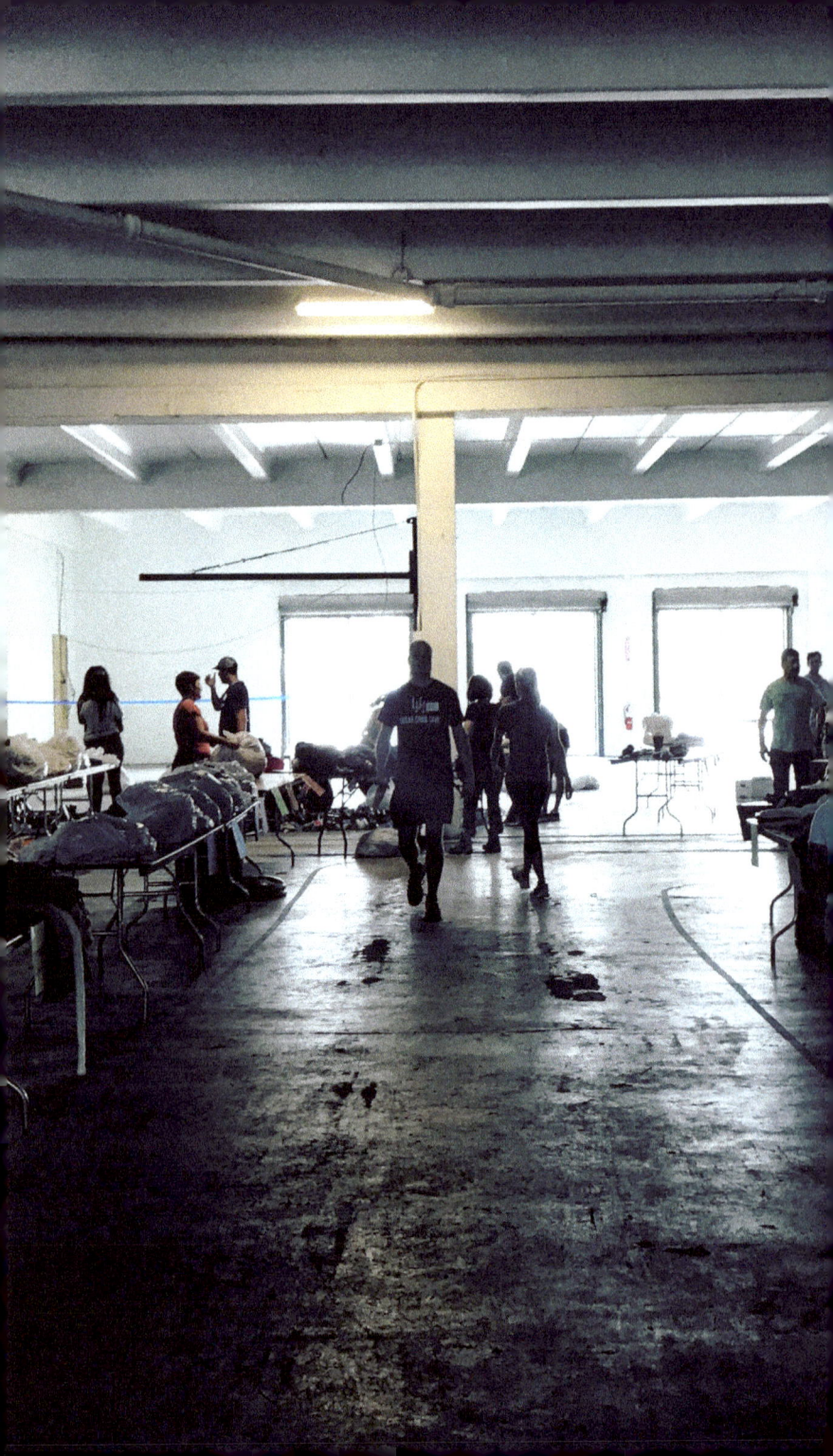

You have it in you.

To serve,

to do good,

to make a difference.

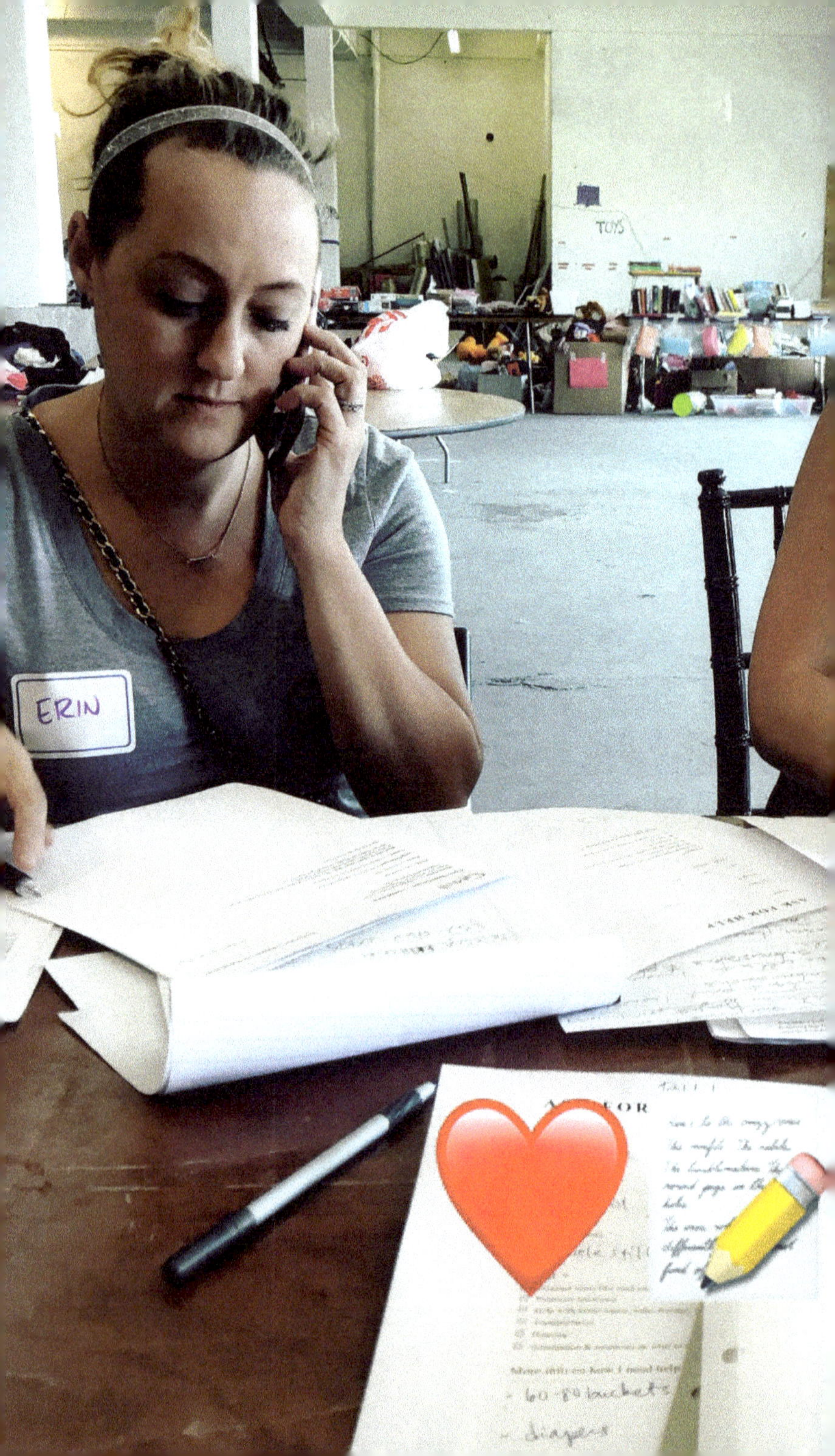
TOYS
ERIN

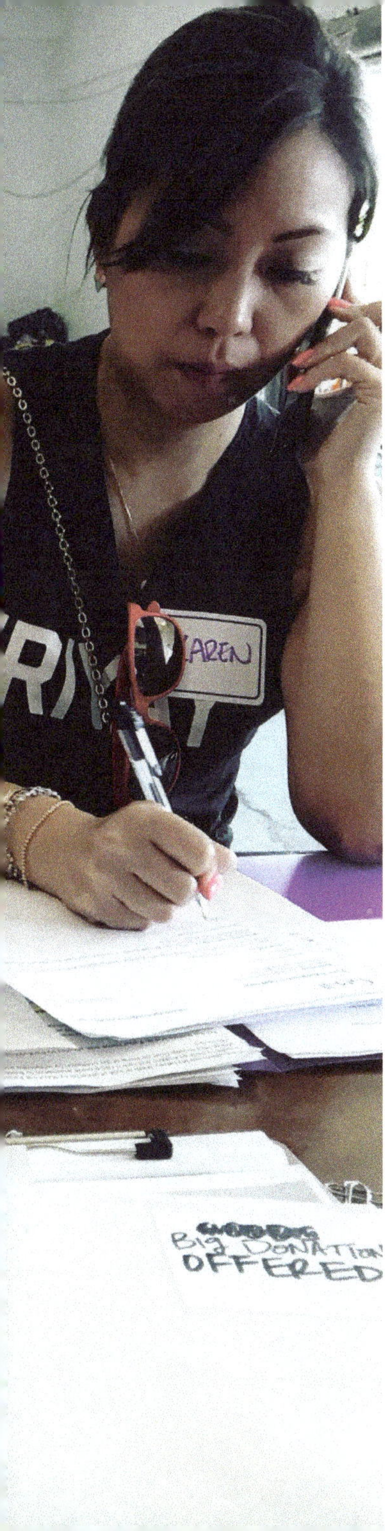
Big DONATION
OFFERED

I know you know an everyday hero.

Your parents, a teacher, a co-worker, a friend.

Let them know that their deeds don't go unnoticed.

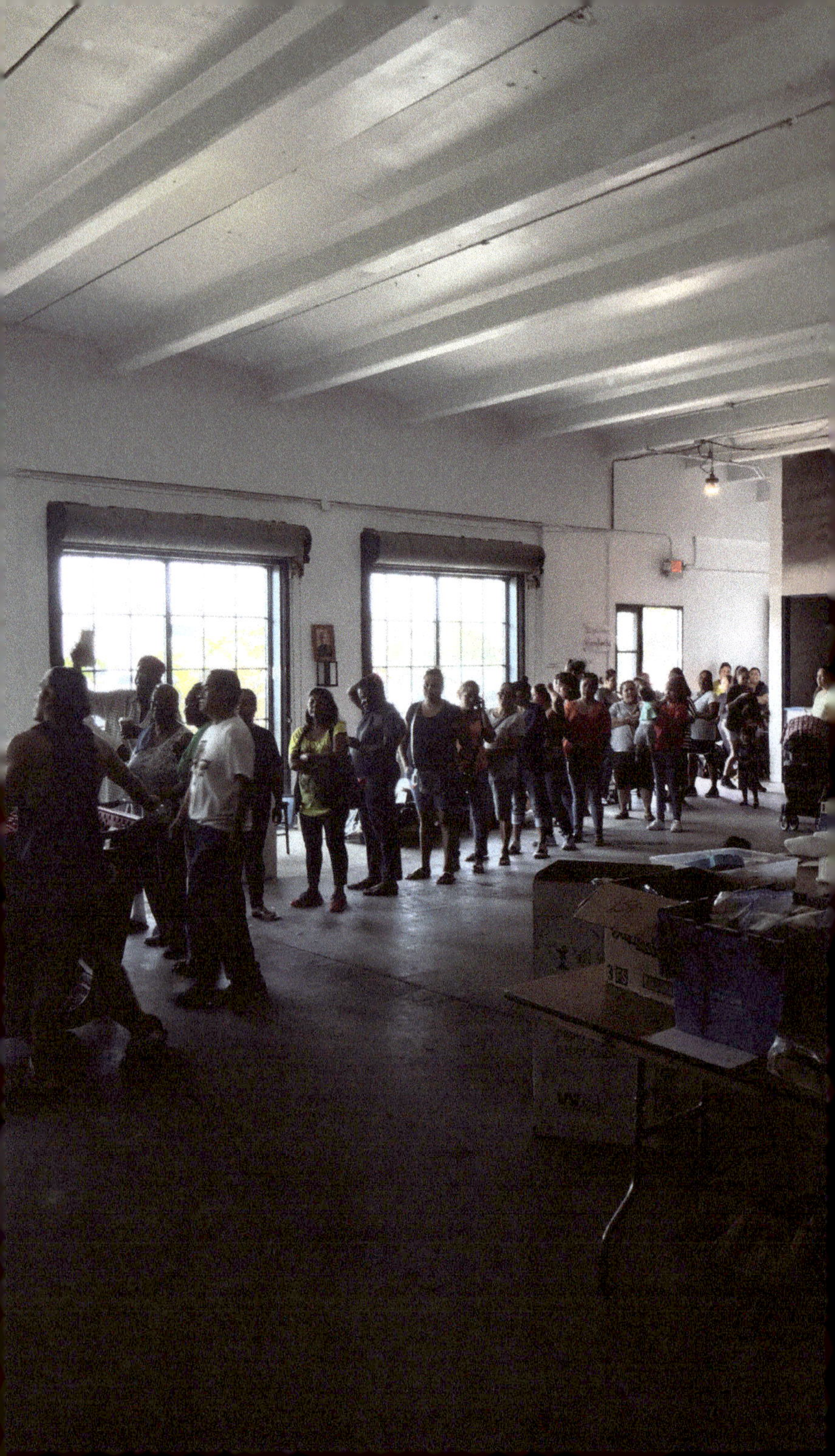

Everyday heroism is not limited to service during catastrophes.

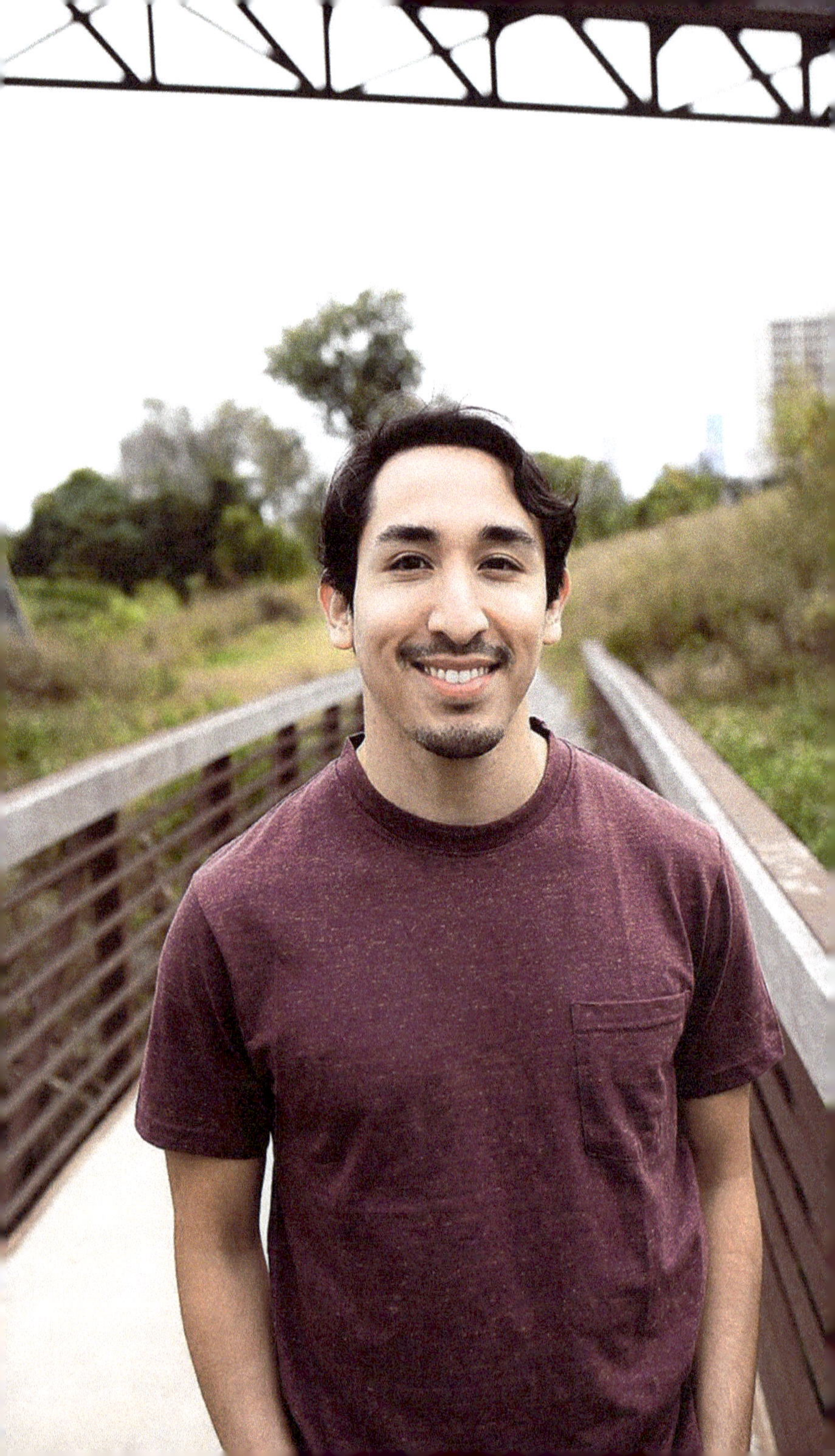

Go out and thank a hero today.
They have you surrounded.

They teach baseball
and music.
They help the ill
and our grandparents.
They foster dogs
and goodwill.

They work for a better planet.

Look around you.

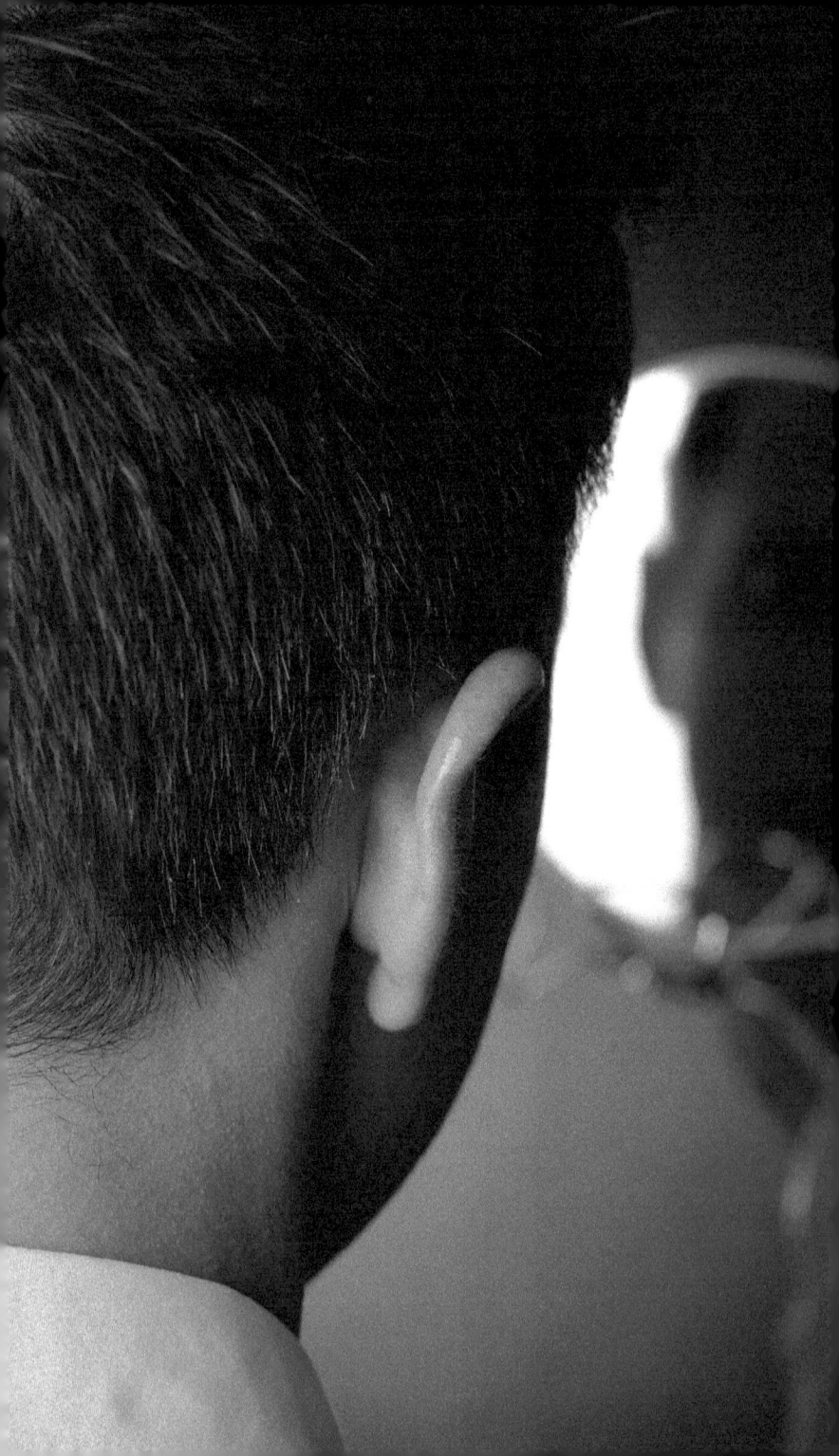

Then,
find the hero
in yourself.

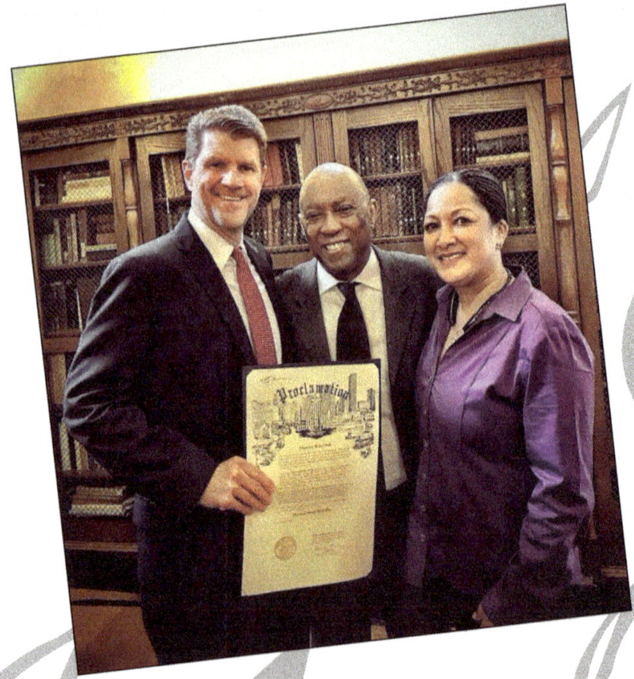

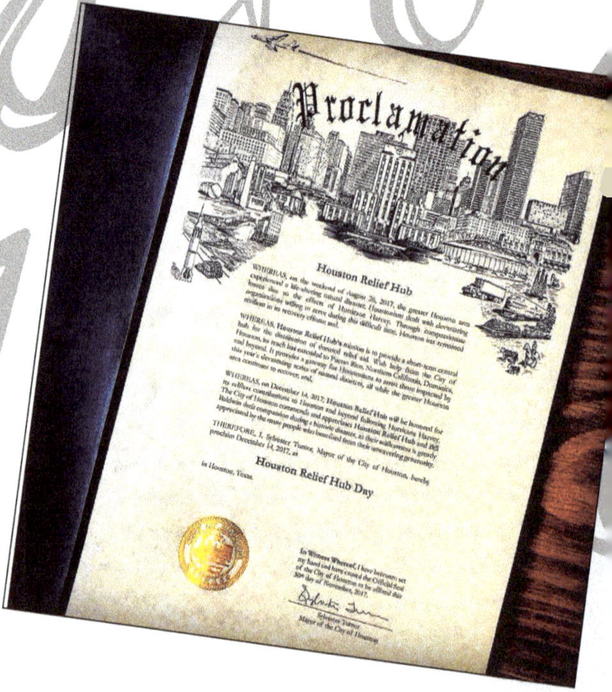

Proclamation

Houston Relief Hub

WHEREAS, on the weekend of August 26, 2017, the greater Houston area experienced a life-altering natural disaster. Houstonians dealt with devastating losses due to the effects of Hurricane Harvey. Through compassionate organizations willing to serve during this difficult time, Houston has remained resilient in its recovery efforts; and,

WHEREAS, Houston Relief Hub's mission is to provide a short-term central hub for the distribution of donated relief aid. With help from the City of Houston, its reach has extended to Puerto Rico, Northern California, Dominica, and beyond. It provides a gateway for Houstonians to assist those impacted by this year's devastating series of natural disasters, all while the greater Houston area continues to recover; and,

WHEREAS, on December 14, 2017, Houston Relief Hub will be honored for its selfless contributions to Houston and beyond following Hurricane Harvey. The City of Houston commends and appreciates Houston Relief Hub and Bill Baldwin their compassion during a historic disaster, as their selflessness is greatly appreciated by the many people who benefited from their unwavering generosity.

THEREFORE, I, Sylvester Turner, Mayor of the City of Houston, hereby proclaim December 14, 2017, as

Houston Relief Hub Day

in Houston, Texas.

In Witness Whereof, I have hereunto set my hand and have caused the Official Seal of the City of Houston to be affixed this 30th day of November, 2017.

Sylvester Turner
Mayor of the City of Houston

No one but you are the everyday heroes
of tomorrow. So go out from here and
simply make some difference.

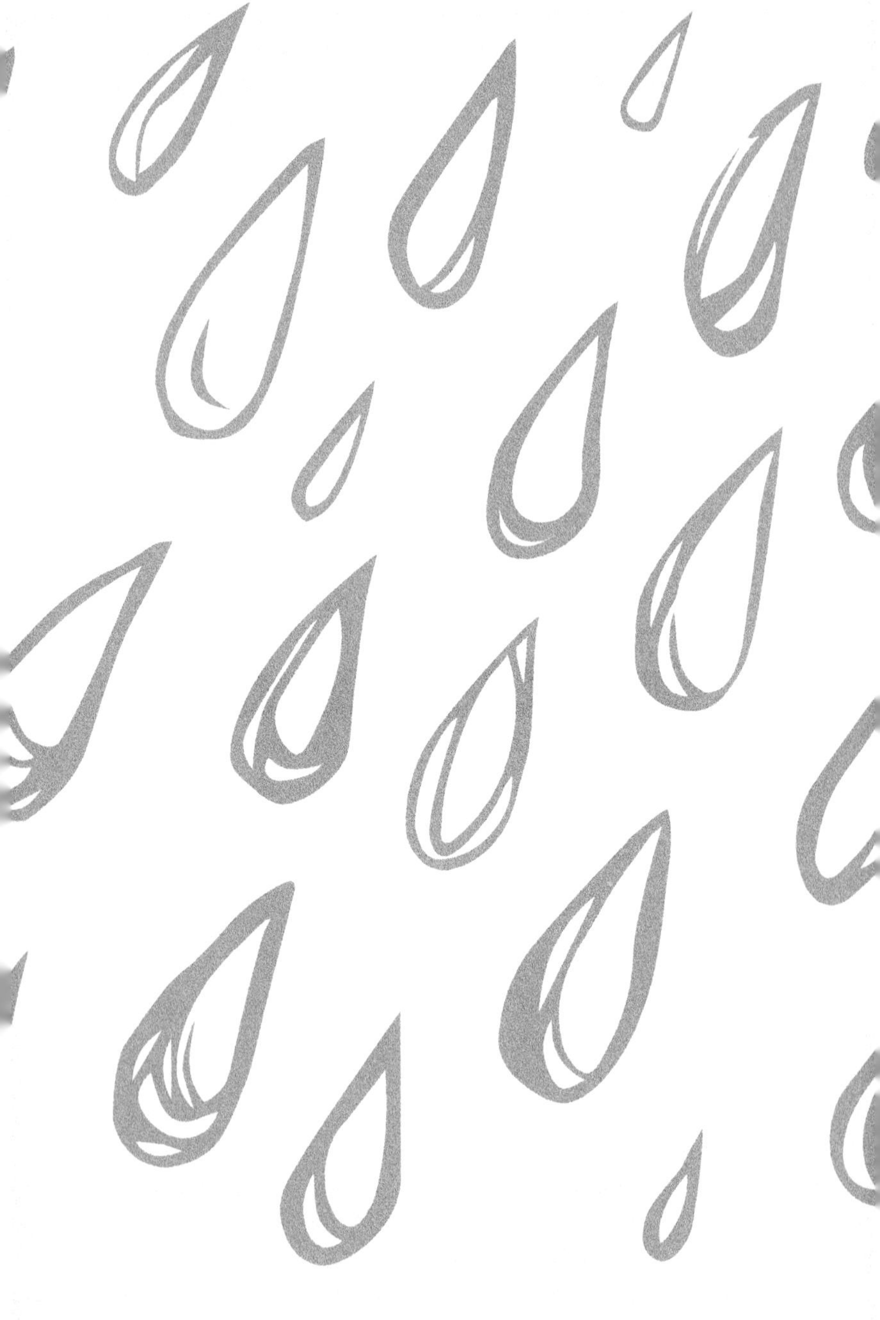

IN APPRECIATION

This book is a dream I had for many years and would not be a reality if not for numerous individuals. There is no way to thank everyone, but I can't let the chance go by not to express my heartfelt appreciation to many.

One of the highlights of my life was the honor of giving the commencement address at Sam Houston State University in the aftermath of Hurricane Harvey. I am so grateful for the invitation from then President Dana Hoyt and the support of longtime friends Rhonda Ellisor and Thelma Mooney, who helped make that happen.

On the very first day of arriving at the George R. Brown, I met and soon formed a lasting bond with Rick Smaile, Erin and Tommy Locke, Chris Brombacher, and Pablo Vega. Any success I had there—and subsequently—was a result of their efforts. I am so grateful for our meeting and for our lasting friendships.

Starting the Harvey Relief Hub was both taxing and straining on my real estate firm, and I will always appreciate the support and understanding of my staff, agents, and clients.

Most of the success we had must be credited to Aaron Flores, who is the most talented individual I know. Without his efforts, neither the Hub nor this book would have happened. I will be eternally grateful to him for so many things.

Mario Castillo started his first day of working for me at the Hub. It was not exactly what he signed up for, but it was a great way for us to get to know one another quickly. He has continued to work on relief efforts as much as me for these last years. He is a real trooper.

After leaving the GRB, when the idea of starting an independent relief effort was just in my head, I went to dinner with State Senator John Whitmire to get his advice. His support gave me the needed confidence to get started. I am grateful for his guidance and Friendship.

Initially, there was doubt and confusion as to whether starting such an effort would in any way hurt the City of Houston's ongoing efforts. The one thing I needed to start the Harvey Relief Hub was the support from Houston Mayor Sylvester Turner. His call in the middle of the aftermath of the storm really did pave the way for our efforts. I will always appreciate his support both for the Hub and his confidence in us to lead the Pay It Forward efforts to Puerto Rico after Hurricane Maria and to the Carolinas following Hurricane Florence.

After the initial relief efforts at the GRB closed down, the city would merge their relief efforts with ours for several months. I also owe a debt of gratitude to Janice Weaver, who constantly reminds us "it's all about the city." She is an everyday hero.

Have a crisis, and you will soon find out who your friends are. With little to no time, I called on Jon

Deal about a location to create the Hub. Without hesitation he not only made the perfect place available, but at a cost to him. This kindness was a huge gift to the citizens of Houston and is very much appreciated.

To my many friends who came and donated, sorted items, and worked at the hub in sweaty and less than desirable conditions— I thank you all.

The operation of the Hub would never have worked without the efforts of my brother John Baldwin, one of the hardest workers I have ever known. His warehouse layout and organization, and forklift operation were instrumental in our success.

Of course, I could not have done any of this without the love and support of my amazing partner, Fady Armanious, who put up with all of this for months and months.

Ginger and Richard, I hope I always make you proud. All of this I do with you in mind and in my heart.

CPSIA information can be obtained
at www.ICGtesting.com
Printed in the USA
BVHW021814010622
638438BV00039B/603/J